THE SPIRIT OF THOREAU

THOREAU ON WATER
Reflecting Heaven

The Spirit of Thoreau

SPONSORED BY THE THOREAU SOCIETY

Wesley T. Mott, Series Editor

Thoreau on Education:
Uncommon Learning

Thoreau on Science:
Material Faith

Thoreau on Mountains:
Elevating Ourselves

Thoreau on Land:
Nature's Canvas

Thoreau on Water:
Reflecting Heaven

THOREAU ON WATER

Reflecting Heaven

Edited by Robert Lawrence France

Foreword by David James Duncan

A Mariner Original

Houghton Mifflin Company

BOSTON   NEW YORK

2001

For information about permission to reproduce selections
from this book, write to Permissions, Houghton Mifflin Company,
215 Park Avenue South, New York, New York 10003.

Visit our Web site: www.houghtonmifflinbooks.com.

Library of Congress Cataloging-in-Publication Data

Thoreau, Henry David, 1817–1862.
    Thoreau on water : reflecting heaven / edited by Robert
Lawrence France ; foreword by David James Duncan.
        p. cm. — (Spirit of Thoreau)
    "A Mariner original."
    Includes bibliographical references.
    ISBN 0-395-95386-3
    1. Thoreau Henry David, 1817–1862 — Quotations.   2. Water
— Quotations, maxims, etc.   I. France, R. L. (Robert Lawrence)
II. Title.

        PS3042. F7 2001
        818'.309—dc21   00-046554

Book design by Anne Chalmers
Type: Bulmer (Monotype)

Printed in the United States of America
QUM 10 9 8 7 6 5 4 3 2 1

Selections from volumes 1–5 of Thoreau's *Journal*
are from *The Writings of Henry David Thoreau*, Witherell, E., ed.
Copyright © 1972 by Princeton University Press. Reprinted
by permission of Princeton University Press.

Contents

———

Foreword

DAVID JAMES DUNCAN

THE TYPICALLY frenetic twenty-first-century American with e-mails to answer, profits to make, and IRAs to fatten might well wonder why he or she would ever want to sit and ponder words set down by some Concord rustic, a half-century before the invention of the horseless carriage, after gazing upon a few bodies of water near his long-since-subdivided home. Here are just three of the hundreds of possible answers to that question:

1. Because ponds "are great crystals on the surface of the earth, Lakes of Light. If they were permanently congealed, and small enough to be clutched, they would, perchance, be carried off by slaves, like precious stones, to adorn the heads of emperors; but being liquid, and ample, and secured to us and our successors forever, we disregard them. They are too pure to have a market value; they contain no muck."
2. Because water "is earth's eye; looking into which the beholder measures the depth of his own nature."

3. Because reflected water "multiplies the heavens" by serving as "a mirror which no stone can crack, whose quicksilver will never wear off, whose gilding Nature continually repairs."

If George Washington is "the Father of Our Country," Henry David Thoreau is the beloved son of it. As he put it himself: "I am made to love the pond & the meadow as the wind is made to ripple the water."

Thoreau was not so much a renegade (as he is remembered, thanks to "Civil Disobedience") as a man unabashedly in love with the earth, fire, water, air, flora, fauna, seasonal symphony, and expanse of his native land. What lent him a renegade air was his faithfulness to these loves at a time when few Americans were expressing anything but lust for the same objects. At the time when Henry David commenced his incomparable journals, most of the Yankee intelligentsia were filing for a permanent divorce between the North American continent and the English language that had come to dominate it, so that they might more rapidly divide and exploit the entire property. Inspired by the Industrial Revolution, by that revolution's pitifully reductive (and thus eminently quotable) philosophers, and by a few conveniently bowdlerized smitches of faux-Bible, these triumphalist "subduers of the land" pretty much ruled the American turf in Henry's day. Thoreau's greatest feat, as I see it, was to set an example of a solitary, anomalous, exquisitely articulated, deeply fulfilling life lived in perfect contradiction to the ruling follies of his day. Henry's days, like the pages of his works, were spent enacting an endless marriage ceremony between the very land and language his neighbors were so busily trying to divide. In so doing, Thoreau changed the North American continent, and the English language, for good.

A single example of an HDT alteration: At the time America was colonized the word "wilderness" (derived from the Old English *wildéor,* a combination of "wild" and "deer") was a highly suspect term indeed. For generations of run-of-the-pew, manifest-destiny-spewing colonists, the word "wild" meant in America what it meant to the British: uncivilized, ungodly, treacherous, pagan, dirty, bloodthirsty, and sexually nasty. And "wilderness" was deemed guilty by association. To enter wilderness in the reverent manner of Thoreau's spiritual heir John Muir was unthinkable in Henry's day. Wilderlands were no place to seek clarity direct from the Creator and creation, unmediated by priests, pundits, and pragmatists. On the contrary, wilderness was the "fallen" and savage chaos that "we the [chosen] people" entered only of necessity, praying to escape with our innocence, sanity, health, personal wealth, pious faith, and cherry intact. (John Bunyan: "Woefully I walk the wilderness of this world." Shakespeare: "Jailed by a wilderness of sea.")

Enter the rusticated, *Gita*-quoting Concord naturalist, with his homemade clothes and pencils, ever-present journal, and perfect willingness not only to perceive wild beauty and to painstakingly articulate even his most intricate perceptions of it, but also to take care (as his contemporary, Charles Darwin, did not) to step inward and away from his ceaseless observations and ratiocinations in order to simply marvel—in a rhapsodic mode formerly made famous by mystics, and later by Muir — at the way natural beauty resonates in, and sheds light upon, the human interior.

The result of this steadfast, lifelong discipline was the salvation not only of a sacred word, but, eventually, of much of the American wildlands the word was meant to signify. In the mid-nineteenth century — even as the U.S. Cavalry (so beloved by Ronald Reagan), along with smallpox, was destroying the last beautiful tribal cultures; as usurping settlers were plowing under the Great Plains; and as the West's buffalo, beaver, eagle, wolf, bear, and "varmint" populations were being shot, trapped, and strychnined for the Betterment of (top-hat-wearing European) Man — Henry David Thoreau gazed awhile westward, then inward, and in his best, most anomalous manner observed, "The West of which I speak is but another name for the Wild; and what I have been preparing to say is, that in wildness is the preservation of the World." And with that unprecedented sentence, the fortunes of our despised, "woeful," John (and Paul!) Bunyan–style "wilderness" began to change.

Henry David Thoreau, it turns out, was the point man for what is now an international legion of biophiles, Greens, virtuous pagans, and earth-adoring altruists. What's more, his two-pronged lifelong habit of acute observation and notation during the long daily saunter, followed by an equally acute engagement with the intricacies of our language back at home, obviated factional strife among our legions by showing us that science *is* art, and art science. Quietly, and almost singlehandedly, this wonderfully independent, deeply eccentric man rescued England's pariah word "wilderness" from the machinations and self-righteous pieties of industrial Europe and restored to it the dignity and allure that wild lands had possessed in the Old Testament, Gospels, Upanishads, *Kalevala,* Ch'an, Zen, Hindu, Buddhist, and Taoist texts, and in every indigenous culture on earth since the beginning of life and time.

I recently thanked Henry for the thousandth time while listening to David Brower being interviewed on the radio. Asked about the Thoreau-rescued word "wildness," Brower began trying to describe his feelings the first time he set eyes upon a wilderness spring, at age six. And though language perhaps failed him, tone of voice and emotion did not. Eighty preposterously eventful years after sighting what he called "all that clean, clear water, coming up out of dirt," Brower's voice *still* trembled with wonder as he described it. Then, like the spring itself, he gave up on English and simply gushed, "I couldn't understand how it could do it!"

For his gigantic investment in this legacy of unadorned wonder, I thank Henry David Thoreau. For helping us see that wildness is pre-American, and will be post-American, because wildness is simply Earth being Earth, I thank him. For driving home the fact that wildness is the Great Tapestry itself, that it is what allows natural selection to naturally select, what allows biodiversity to diversify, that "wildness" is, then, literally "our mother," I thank him. For seeing first, and so clearly, that the land and its flora are our mother's body and clothes, that the seas, rivers, ponds are her organs, veins, arteries, that every inch of her is holy, and that the man, woman, or child who strives to defend her living parts and life — even in poverty or political impotence, even against seemingly hopeless odds — is not only a hero but an integral part of her, hence every bit as holy as that which they seek to defend, I thank him.

I thank Henry Thoreau the way I thank Earth herself: season by season, again and again, ever more gratefully.

Lolo, Montana
　　July 2000

Introduction

Water indeed reflects heaven *because my mind does — such is its serenity — its transparency — & stillness.... Standing on distant hills you see the* heavens reflected *the evening sky in some low lake or river in the valley — as perfectly as in any mirror they could be — Does it not prove how intimate heaven is with earth?*

—31 August–1 September 1851, *Journal*

ONE OF Henry David Thoreau's principal goals was to achieve harmony in his life with nature. He constantly sought to find a practical balance between a contemplative spiritual life and an active physical existence, and his particular genius came from living out what others, such as Ralph Waldo Emerson and Bronson Alcott, only speculated about. By exploring a locality in more detail than few have ever done, before or since, Thoreau became master of the microcosm. Always he was driven by the pressing need to join naturalistic insight with ethical and aesthetic idealization. Although volumes have been written about Thoreau's motivations for the grand experiment of his life, which represents, perhaps even more than his writings, his greatest contribution and legacy, his walking companion and first biographer, William Channing, may have best expressed it when he wrote that

Thoreau was simply "alive from top to bottom with curiosity."

Of all landscapes, aquatic ones were those that most inspired Thoreau. "The water on a lake, from however distant a point seen, is always the centre of the landscape," he emphasized. He felt his life to be bounded by water, from his first childhood memories of being taken to visit Walden Pond to his deathbed reflections upon the rain against the windowpanes. With its abundance of varied bodies of water, Concord was the ideal environment in which Thoreau could develop his hydrophilic leanings: "It is well to have some water in your neighborhood, to give buoyancy to and float the earth."

Thoreau's study of water — and of nature generally — evolved through four stages or perspectives: nature idolized, nature idealized, nature itemized, and nature lionized. He did not, however, simply shift from one perspective to another, but constantly circled back to employ several or all simultaneously. Briefly, for "nature idolized," Thoreau drew upon the concepts of transcendental contemplation that his friend, neighbor, and teacher Emerson expounded. "Nature idealized," representing Thoreau's aesthetic appreciation of nature, developed from his reading of landscape painters, European Romantics, and Native American and Hindu cosmology. By applying the scientific philosophy of Alexander von Humboldt, Thoreau engaged in the empirical natural history of "nature itemized." Having idolized, idealized, and itemized nature, Thoreau inevitably came to recognize the environmental problems presented by human relationships with nature, and he asked questions about how to solve these problems, pursuing the topic with vigor later in life as he lionized or championed and defended nature.

This volume focuses on the first two categories of Thoreau's relationship with nature — idolization and idealization — in regard to water. The subtitle, *Reflecting Heaven*, represents the kind of word trick that Thoreau loved, for it refers to both spiritual and physical reflections. In the first sense, water serves as a stimulus to reflections about divinity, soul, and society — "looking into which the beholder measures the depth of his own nature." In the second sense, the reflecting sky highlights the beauty of the earth — "heaven is under our feet as well as over our heads."

I have grouped the quotations, which are drawn from all of Thoreau's works, by the type of water body he was writing about — ephemeral waters and wetlands; rivers and streams; lakes and ponds; and seacoast. Within each type, Thoreau's observations are further divided by category of experience, and within those categories the quotations are arranged chronologically.

Ecopsychology: Believing As Seeing

Reading any of Thoreau's writing, most particularly his two-million-word *Journal*, leaves an overwhelming impression of his modernity. Indeed, he seems to have anticipated much of modern scientific thought, including the new field of ecopsychology, which explores the relations between the outside world and that within. As Barry Lopez writes: "I think of two landscapes — one outside the self, the other within. The external landscape is the one we see.... The interior landscape responds to the character and subtlety of an exterior landscape; the shape of the individual mind is affected by land as it is by genes." This is the theme behind Simon Schama's seminal *Landscape and Memory,* which begins with a quotation from Thoreau's *Journal* for 30 August 1856: "It is vain to dream of a wildness distant from ourselves. There is none such. It is the bog in our brains and bowels, the primitive vigor of Nature in us, that inspires that dream. I shall never find in the wilds of Labrador any greater wildness than in some recess of Concord, i.e. than I import into it."

Many of Thoreau's pioneering ecological insights, integrating both transcendental and aesthetic reflections, were inspired by water. As Laura Sewall writes in her book *Sight and Sensibility: The Ecopsychology of Perception,* "Seeing archetypal dimensions in the landscape is a reflection of the psyche, the soul found within *both* the observer and the landscape itself. The reflection of the personal psyche becomes especially apparent with careful observation of the world soul — when one looks toward the familiar mountain, toward the forms with which one is aligned. The changes in one's response, from one day to the next, reflect the changing of the personal psyche more than that of the mountain. In this sense, the landscape becomes a clear mirror in which the individual psyche is seen in what is seen — reflected back with the twined powers of vision and imagination. And in the process, with this way of seeing, the world becomes ensouled." Achieving such heavenly reflections was Thoreau's intention in his use of water to conjoin visual and mental images, metaphors and lessons, deep in the very "bog in our brains and bowels." His choice of the word "bog" speaks volumes about the importance of water to his perception of the world and his (and our) place within it.

Seeking Higher Laws

Transcendentalists advocated a process of translation whereby matter is converted into spirit, and nature is used as a tool to foster reflection, which in turn leads to revelation of "higher truths." Nature here is imbued with symbolic meaning, and the key to cracking its divine mystery is to use the skills of the poet: imagery, trope, and metaphor. Landscape provides an impetus for illumination and spiritual instruction, by which receptive individuals can range far: "In the spaces of thought are the reaches of land and water, where men go and come. The landscape lies far and fair within, and the deepest thinker is the farthest travelled."

Though he later broke away somewhat, Thoreau initially embraced Emerson's transcendentalist belief that nature is the externalization of the mind, mind the internalization of nature, and that the true perfection of nature is accessible only to the higher mental faculties of reason and imagination. There is a reciprocity between the emergent properties of nature and the emergent wisdom of the perceiving mind, of "nature looking into nature."

Nature's Divinity

"What in other men is religion is in me a love of nature," Thoreau claimed. In his efforts to attain mystic insight, however, he always had difficulty reconciling an attitude of abandon with one of attentive watchfulness. In his pantheistic "worship" of nature, Thoreau sought knowledge and clarity of mind rather than grace and ecstatic transport: "My profession is to be always on the alert to find God in nature — to know his lurking places. To attend all the oratorios — the operas in nature." *Walden,* in a sense, can be regarded as an instruction manual for moving toward a higher life. *A Week on the Concord and Merrimack Rivers,* which contains Thoreau's most transcendental writing, is structured as a sort of aqueous *Pilgrim's Progress,* with the journeyer moving upstream and temporally backward to the time when his traveling companion, his beloved brother, was still alive. Divinity is attained through water: "Man flows at once to God when the channel of purity is open." Thoreau progressed from the ancient Greek maxim of "know thyself" to his own version of "explore thyself."

Mirrors to the Soul

In his first journal Thoreau entered this quotation from a French dictionary: "From the primitive word Ver, signifying water ... is derived the word verite; for as water, by reason of its transparency and limpidness, is the mirror of bodies — of physical êtres, so also is truth equally the mirror of ideas — intellectual êtres, representing them in a manner as faithful and clear, as the water does a physical body." For Thoreau, then, the transparency of lakes and ponds served as a metaphor for the purity of humanity's own nature. Heaven's grace is offered to us as a mirrored reflection of our own elevated divinity. A pond such as Walden provides a grounding of heaven on earth, and offers spiritual possibilities to one who lives in proximity to it. Rivers, on the other hand, are works in progress, highways to spiritual maturation, providing restorative uplift along the way. The ocean, finally, is the grand transpersonal consciousness from which we were separated at birth.

Above all, it was Walden Pond that anchored Thoreau, giving him a base from which to reflect upon his world. "What I have observed of the pond is no less true in ethics," he wrote in *Walden*. Plumbing the depths of the pond, he explored the depths of his own soul: "My nature may be as still as this water, but it is not so pure, and its reflections are not so distinct." Walden Pond, "the distiller of celestial dews," like Thoreau himself, was a spiritual traveler, and its evaporation back into the atmosphere, like Thoreau's writing, carried its message farther afield.

Thoreau's river journey in *A Week* is as much a mental outing as a physical one. Rivers symbolize the search for the regenerative powers of nature: "Who hears the rippling of the rivers will not utterly despair of anything"; and "A man's life should be as fresh as a river. It should be the same channel, but a new water every instant." Rivers are symbols of Thoreau's most profound desires and experiences, in that they not only transport our bodies but also "conduct our thoughts."

Carrying Darwinism to its extreme, Thoreau speculated that man is an evolved "product of sea-slime," with the ocean representing our original haven. Standing on the outer coast of Cape Cod, the rest of the troubled continent behind him, he stared repeatedly at the open ocean, where, he believed, one could float free of all earthly problems, returning to some sort of original womb. But just as birth is a violent process, Thoreau acknowledged the savageness of the ocean wilderness with the same mute awe and trepidation as he did the dense uncivilized Maine woods he spied from the top of Mount Katahdin.

Nature as Existence Rather than Symbol

To Emerson and other transcendentalists, nature was a resource; in order to be interesting, it had to be connected to the human soul. The transcendentalists often placed little value on the inherent properties of nature itself, extolling only its emergent properties and their utility for contemplation. It was inevitable that Thoreau would deviate from this line of thought, finding divinity by looking deeper into nature rather than into its effects on our minds. For him, transcendental knowledge was never a satisfactory substitute for direct experience. Nature for Thoreau was not an abstract veil to be pushed aside on the way to enlightenment, but rather a real and tangible entity worthy of attention regardless of our anthropocentric desires for higher meaning. Neither symbol nor allegory, nature was the very essence of existence, whose workings had purpose whether or not humans were around to appreciate them.

Senses Employed

Sometimes, particularly on his night walks, the intense beauty of nature would be so intoxicating that Thoreau would be drawn to the border of the spiritual. At such times he would abandon his increasing scientific imperative to record nature's minutiae and instead simply revel in pure wonder at the reflecting patterns of moonlight over the water. Bothered by the poverty of objective scientific investigation, he let his eyes lead him to an appreciation of the world: "A man sees only what concerns him.... How much more, then, it requires different intentions of the eye and mind to attend to different departments of knowledge! How differently the poet and the naturalist look at objects." His clarion cry became, "Employ your senses!" He believed that sustained visual attention was the most natural approach: "I suspect that the child plucks its first flower with an insight into its beauty and significance which the subsequent botanist never retains." Nevertheless, he was cautious about completely abandoning himself to the sense of wonder, lest his soul become overwhelmed and his poetic faculties become dissipated.

Thoreau was drawn to reflections of light on water, with their myriad simultaneous images and colors. He attempted to heighten his experience by what he called "a true sauntering of the eye" rather than a direct stare: "Mem. Try this experiment again; i.e. look not toward nor from the sun but athwart this line." He would squint through his eyelashes or, in at least one instance, view the world through his legs: "I look between my legs up the river across Fair Haven. Subverting the head, we refer things to the heavens; the sky becomes the ground of the picture, and where the river breaks through the low hills which slope to meet each other.... Perhaps there is some advantage in looking at the landscape this way." Unknowingly, Thoreau was following a technique taught more than five hundred years earlier by the Zen master Kigen Dogen, who instructed his students in new ways of viewing the world by "presenting sideways and using upside down," or what Laura Sewall refers to as "reversing the world." For Thoreau, such optical gymnastics led to increased perception through deliberately indirect observation. Like a metaphysical poet, he sought to jar us into a recognition of the uniqueness of the mundane that we have become inured to, spurring us to re-sense and re-experience the world around us.

Visualizing the Landscape

Thoreau looked at landscapes the way many nineteenth-century landscape painters did. He frequently spoke of "prospects" and of "framing" views. But unlike Frederic Church and many painters of the Hudson River School, who tended to work on the grandiose scale of the sublime, Thoreau preferred the smaller view of the picturesque. In this he drew inspiration from reading William Gilpin, an eighteenth-century painter and writer who championed the rugged irregularity of the picturesque over the smoothed regularity of the beautiful. From Gilpin, Thoreau learned that the play of physical light and shadow can nurture the human soul by causing pleasure or pain without any suggestion of morality or divinity.

Thoreau's view of the visual landscape was also shaped by John Ruskin's *Elements of Drawing,* a book that would later inspire the Impressionists. He embraced Ruskin's thesis that phenomenological sight was more important than experiential drawing: "How much of beauty — of color, as well as form — on which our eyes daily rest goes unperceived by us! No one botanist is likely to distinguish nicely the different shades of green with which the open surface of the earth is clothed — not even a landscape painter if he does not know the species of sedges and grasses which paint it." Not through scientific abstraction but through his heightened capacity to see what is real and significant, Thoreau developed what Laura Walls refers to as an "epistemology of contact." He was interested "in not what you look at—but how you look and whether you see." It was the cool blues and azures found predominantly in sky reflected in the water that rendered Thoreau most rapturous. The sense of limitless space that these colors suggested was a mirror of his far-ranging thoughts about his own psyche.

Nature's Grand Fluidity

The picturesque, however, was not enough for Thoreau. He criticized Gilpin's narrow and static view of nature as viewscape, envisioning instead a dynamic nature as force, process, and energy. Even when immersed in the scientism of his later years, Thoreau, inspired by the writings of Goethe and Wordsworth, maintained his Romantic belief in the grand, almost spiritual, organic cycle of nature. To him all nature was a miracle, the ordinary capable of being elevated to myth, and everything ecologically intertwined. Like St. Francis, he embraced the idea that humans were nothing special. Instead, nature was a vast community of equals, as Native American and Hindu cosmology taught. Nature was neither sublime nor picturesque but was rather the embodiment of the universal spirit. In breaking with traditional transcendentalism, Thoreau saw nature as a sensate reality rather than as a symbol of something else, and he spent his life searching for the mysterious force that bound all nature together through time. He believed in a vibrant earth similar to the ancient Greek concept of Gaia, which has become popular today.

For Thoreau, the most important force that held this

grand vision of nature together was a stream of "some invisible fluid." The earth "is not a dead, inert mass, it is a body, has a spirit, is organic, is fluid to the influence of its spirit, and to whatever particle of that spirit is in me." He viewed nature, therefore, as a grand pattern of aqueous circulation. He referred to rivers of sap, of stars, of rock and ore, of birds, and spoke of thoughts as streams of consciousness. Water bodies to Thoreau were alive — rivers were earth's "veins," ponds were "earth's eyes," and Walden Pond represented the "blue navel" of the world around which he circulated.

⁓

Reading a book, no matter how inspiring, is no substitute for direct experience. Knowing this, Thoreau would certainly have encouraged you to place this slim volume in a pocket or a backpack and head outdoors to a pond, river, wetland, or the ocean. There, with his quotations beside you, and perhaps accompanied by a journal in which to capture your own musings, magic may happen, as it has for thousands the world over for the last century: "The refractive property of water ensures that when we look in deep, we see shallow. When we gaze down, searching for some shadowy profundity below the surface, what usually comes back to us is mearly us" (Jonathan Raban); and "Water reflects not only clouds and trees and cliffs, but all the infinite variations of mind and spirit we bring to it" (Sigurd Olson). Therefore, go out and watch sparkling light and dancing waves, and reflect, as Thoreau and many others did before him.

Thoreau on Water

Ephemeral Waters
and Wetlands

―――――

NATURE IDOLIZED
Instead of looking into the sky, I look into the placid reflecting water for the signs and promise of the morrow.

Sometimes this purer and cooler water, bursting out from under a pine or a rock, was collected into a basin close to the edge of, and level with the river, a fountain-head of the Merrimack. So near along life's stream are the fountains of innocence and youth making fertile its sandy margin; and the voyageur will do well to replenish his vessels often at these uncontaminated sources. Some youthful spring, perchance, still empties with tinkling music into the oldest river, even when it is falling into the sea, and we imagine that its music is distinguished by the river gods from the general lapse of the stream, and falls sweeter on their ears in proportion as it is nearer to the ocean. As the evaporations of the river feed thus these unsuspected springs which filter through its banks, so, perchance, our aspirations fall back again in springs on the margin of life's stream to refresh and purify it. The yellow and tepid river may float his scow, and cheer his eye with its reflections and its ripples, but the boatman quenches his thirst at this small rill alone. It is this purer and cooler element that chiefly sustains his life. The race will long survive that is thus discreet.

A Week, 193–94

Innumerable little streams overlap and interlace one with another, exhibiting a sort of hybrid product, which obeys half way the law of currents, and half way that of vegetation. As it flows it takes the form of sappy leaves or vines, making heaps of pulpy sprays a foot or more in depth, and resembling . . . the laciniated lobed and imbricated thalluses of some lichens; or you are reminded of coral, of leopards' paws or birds' feet, of brains or lungs or bowels, and excrements of all kinds . . .

When I see on the one side the inert bank . . . and on the other this luxuriant foliage, the creation of an hour, I am affected as if in a peculiar sense I stood in the laboratory of the Artist who made the world and me, — had come to where he was still at work, sporting on this bank, and with excess of energy strewing his fresh designs about. I feel as if I were nearer to the vitals of the globe, for this sandy overflow is something such a foliaceous mass as the vitals of the animal body. You find thus in the very sands an anticipation of the vegetable leaf.

Walden, 305–6

How refreshing the sound of the smallest waterfall in hot weather — I sit by that on Clematis brook and listen to its music — The very sight of this half stagnant pond hole drying up & leaving bare mud — with the pollywogs &

turtles making off in it is agreeable & encouraging to behold as if it contained the seeds of life — the liquor rather
boiled down. The foulest water will bubble purely. They
speak to our blood even these stagnant slimy pools. It too
no doubt has its falls nobler than Montmorenci —
grander than Niagara in the course of its circulations —
Here is the primitive force of egypt and the Nile — where
the lotus grows.

15 June 1852, Journal 5: 99

The distant view of the open flooded Sudbury meadows
all dark blue surrounded by a landscape of white snow
gave an impulse to the dormant sap in my veins. Dank
dark blue & angry waves contrasting with the white but
melting winter landscape   Ponds of course do not yet
afford this water prospect — only the flooded meadows.
There is no ice over or near the stream & the flood has
covered or broken up much of the ice on the meadows.
The aspect of these waters at sunset when the air is still
begins to be unspeakably soothing & promising. Waters
are at length and begin to reflect — and instead of looking
into the sky I look into the placid reflecting water for the
signs & promise of the morrow. These meadows are the
most of ocean that I have fairly learned. Now when the
sap of the trees is probably beginning to flow — the sap of
the earth — the river over flows & bursts its icey fetters —

8 March 1853, Journal 5: 475

How much would be subtracted from the day if the water
was taken away! This liquid transparency, of melted
snows partially warmed, spread over the russet surface of
the earth! It is certainly important that there be some

priests, some worshippers of Nature. I do not imagine anything going on to-day away from and out of sight of the waterside.

9 April 1855, *Journal* VIII: 264

NATURE IDEALIZED
Our vernal lakes have a beauty to my mind which they would not possess if they were more permanent.

And I forgot to say that after I reach the road by Potters barns — or further by potters Brook — I saw the moon sudden reflected full from a pool — A puddle from which you may see the moon reflected — & the earth dissolved under your feet.

The magical moon with attendant stars suddenly looking up with mild lustre from a window in the dark earth.

13 June 1851, *Journal* 3: 260

A little brook crossing the road (the Corner road), a few inches' depth of transparent water rippling over yellow sand and pebbles, the pure blood of nature. How miraculously crystal-like, how exquisite, fine, and subtle, and liquid this element, which an imperceptible inclination in the channel causes to flow thus surely and swiftly! How obedient to its instinct, to the faintest suggestion of the hills! If inclined but a hair's breadth, it is in a torrent haste to obey. And all the revolutions of the planet — nature is so exquisitely adjusted — and the attraction of the stars do not disturb this equipoise, but the rills still flow the same way, and the water levels are not disturbed.

23 July 1851, *Journal* II: 339–40

Here is a little brook of very cold spring water rising a few rods distant with a gray sandy & pebbly bottom — flowing through this dense swampy thicket — where nevertheless the sun falls in here & there between the leaves and shines on its bottom — meandering exceedingly — & sometimes running underground — The trilliums on its brink have fallen into it & bathe their red berries in the water waving in the stream — The water has the coldness it acquired in the bowels of the earth. Here is a recess apparently never frequented — thus this rill flowed here a thousand years ago & with exactly these environments. It is a few rods of primitive wood — such as the bear & the deer beheld — It has a singular charm for me carrying me back in imagination to those days — Yet a fisherman has once found out this retreat & here is his box in the brook to keep his minnows in, now gone to decay. I love the rank smells of the swamp — its decaying leaves. The clean dark-green leaves of the fever-bush overhang the stream —

19 August 1852, *Journal* 5: 302

Close under the lee of the button-bushes which skirt the pond, as I look south, there is a narrow smooth strip of water, silvery and contrasting with the darker rippled body of the pond. Its edge, or the separation between this, which I will call the polished silvery border of the pond, and the dark and ruffled body, is not a straight line or film, but an ever-varying, irregularly and finely serrated or fringed border, ever changing as the breeze falls over the bushes at an angle more or less steep, so that this moment it is a rod wide, the next not half so much. Every feature is thus fluent in the landscape.

14 May 1853, *Journal* V: 154–55

I see the green surface of the meadows and the water through the trees, sparkling with bright reflections. Men will go further and pay more to see a tawdry picture on canvas, a poor painted scene, than to behold the fairest or grandest scene that nature ever displays in their immediate vicinity, though they may have never seen it in their lives.

2 June 1853, *Journal* V: 217

In the spaces of still open water I see the reflection of the hills and woods, which for so long I have not seen, and it gives expression to the face of nature. The face of nature is lit up by these reflections in still water in the spring.

9 March 1854, *Journal* VI: 159

This dark-blue water is the more interesting because it is not a permanent feature in the landscape.

6 May 1854, *Journal* VI: 239

My eyes are attracted to the level line where the water meets the hills now, in time of flood, converting that place into a virgin or temporary shore. There is no strand, — nothing worn; but if it is calm we fancy the water slightly heaped above this line, as when it is poured gently into a goblet.

7 May 1854, *Journal* VI: 242

This season of rain and superabundant moisture makes attractive many an unsightly hollow and recess. I see some roadside lakes, where the grass and clover had already sprung, owing to previous rain or melted snow, now filled with perfectly transparent April rainwater, through which I see to their emerald bottoms, — paved with emerald. In the pasture beyond Nut Meadow Brook Crossing, the unsightly holes where rocks have been dug and blasted out are now converted into perfect jewels. They are filled with water of crystalline transparency, paved with the same emerald, with a few hardhacks and meadow-sweets standing in them, and jagged points of rock, and a few skaters gliding over them. Even these furnish goblets and vases of perfect purity to hold the dews and rains, and what more agreeable bottom can we look to than this which the earliest moisture and sun had tinged green? We do not object to see dry leaves and withered grass at the bottom of the goblet when we drink, if these manifestly do not affect the purity of the water. What wells can be more charming? If I see an early grasshopper drowning in one, it looks like a fate to be envied. Here is no dark unexplored bottom, with its imagined monsters and mud, but perfect sincerity, setting off all that it reveals. Through this medium we admire even the decaying leaves and sticks at the bottom.

24 April 1856, *Journal* VIII: 304–5

Not only meadows but potato and rye fields are buried deep, and you see there, sheltered by the hills on the northwest, a placid blue bay having the russet hills for shores. This kind of bay, or lake, made by the freshet — these deep and narrow "fiords" — can only be seen along such a stream as this, liable to an annual freshet. The water rests as gently as a dewdrop on a leaf, laving its tender temporary shores. It has no strand, leaves no permanent water-mark, but though you look at it a quarter of a mile off, you know that the rising flood is gently overflowing a myriad withered green blades there in succession. There is the magic of lakes that come and go. The lake or bay is not an institution, but a phenomenon. You plainly see that it is so much water poured into the hollows of the earth.

16 March 1859, *Journal* XII: 52

How charming the contrast of land and water, especially a temporary island in the flood, with its new and tender shores of waving outline, so withdrawn yet habitable, above all if it rises into a hill high above the water and contrasting with it the more, and if that hill is wooded, suggesting wildness! Our vernal lakes have a beauty to my mind which they would not possess if they were more permanent. Everything is in rapid flux here, suggesting that Nature is alive to her extremities and superficies.

28 March 1859, *Journal* XII: 95–96

NATURE IDOLIZED
That mirror, as it were a permanent picture to be seen there, a permanent piece of idealism…

The seasons which we seem to *live* in anticipation of is arrived — the water indeed reflects heaven because my mind does — such is its own serenity — its transparency — & stillness.

31 August 1851, *Journal* 4: 24

Sitting by the Spruce swamp in Conant's Grove, I am reminded that this is a perfect day to visit the swamps, with its damp mistling, mildewy air, so solemnly still.

28 September 1851, *Journal* 4: 109

James P Brown's retired pond now shallow & more than half dried up — Seems far away and rarely visited — known to few — though not far off. It is encircled by an amphitheater of low hills on two opposite sides covered with high pine woods — the other sides with young white oaks & white pines respectively I am affected by beholding there reflected this grey day — so unpretendly the gray stems of the Pine wood on the hill side & the sky — that mirror as it were a permanent picture to be seen there — a permanent piece of idealism — What were these reflections to the cows alone! Were these things made for cows' eyes mainly? You shall go over behind the hills, where you would suppose that otherwise there was no eye to behold — & find this piece of magic a constant phenomenon there. It is not merely a few distinguished lakes or pools that reflect the trees & skies but the obscurest pond hole in the most unfrequented dell does the same.

These reflections suggest that the sky underlies the hills as well as overlies them, and in another sense than in appearance

I am a little surprised on beholding this reflection — which I did not perceive for some minutes after looking into the pond — as if I had not regarded this as a constant phenomenon. — What has become of nature's common sense & love of facts when in the very mud puddles she reflects the skies & trees. Does that procedure recommend itself entirely to the common sense of men.? Is that the way the New England farmer would have arranged it?

9 November 1851, *Journal* 4: 171

Nature Idealized

*The attractive point is that line where the water
meets the land.*

It is a strongly marked enduring natural line which in
summer reminds me that the water has once stood over
where I walk   Sometimes the grooved trees tell the same
tale. The wrecks of the meadow which fill a thousand
coves and tell a thousand tales to those who can read
them   Our prairial mediterranean shore. The gentle rise
of water around the trees in the meadow — where oaks &
maples stand far out in the sea — And young elms sometimes are seen standing close around some rocks which
lifts its head above the water — as if protecting it prevent-
ing it from being washed away though in truth they owe
their origin and preservation to it. It first invited & detained their seed & now preserves the soil in which they
grow. A pleasant reminiscence of the rise of waters   To
go up one side of the river & down the other following
this way which meanders so much more than the river itself — If you cannot go on the ice — you are then gently
compelled to take this course which is on the whole more
beautiful — to follow the sinuosities of the meadow. Between the highest water mark & the present water line is
a space generally from a few feet to a few rods in width.

12 February 1851, *Journal* 3: 188

The attractive point is that line where the water meets the
land. — not distinct but known to exist. The willows are
not the less interesting because of their nakedness below.
How rich like what we love to read of South American
primitive forests is the scenery of this river — What luxu-

riance of weeds— What depth of mud along its sides! These old antehistoric-geologic-antediluvian rocks— which only primitive wading birds are worthy to tread—

31 August 1851, *Journal* 4: 23–24

The water on the meadows is now quite high— on account of the melting snow & the rain. It makes a lively prospect when the wind blows— Where our summer meads spread—a tumultuous sea—a myriad waves breaking with white caps, like gambolling sheep— for want of other comparison in the country. Far & wide a sea of motion— schools of porpoises—lines of Virgil realized— One would think it a novel sight for inland meadows—where the cranberry—& andromeada & swamp white oak & maple grow— here is a mimic sea— with its gulls. At the bottom of the sea cranberries.

16 April 1852, *Journal* 4: 456

Beck Stow's Swamp! What an incredible spot to think of in town or city! When life looks sandy and barren, is reduced to its lowest terms, we have no appetite, and it has no flavor, then let me visit such a swamp as this, deep and impenetrable, where the earth quakes for a rod around you at every step, with its open water where the swallows skim and twitter, its meadow and cotton-grass, its dense patches of dwarf andromeda, now brownish-green, with clumps of blueberry bushes, its spruces and its verdurous border of woods imbowering it on every side.

17 July 1852, *Journal* IV: 231

Rivers and Streams

NATURE IDOLIZED

You could anywhere run across the stream on the rocks, and its constant murmuring would quiet the passions of mankind forever.

It required some rudeness to disturb with our boat the mirror-like surface of the water, in which every twig and blade of grass was so faithfully reflected; too faithfully indeed for art to imitate, for only nature may exaggerate herself. The shallowest still water is unfathomable. Wherever the trees and skies are reflected there is more than Atlantic depth, and no danger of fancy running aground. We noticed that it required a separate intention of the eye, a more free and abstracted vision, to see the reflected trees and the sky, than to see the river bottom merely; and so are there manifold visions in the direction of every object, and even the most opaque reflect the heavens from their surface. Some men have their eyes naturally intended to the one, and some to the other object.

A Week, 48

Two men in a skiff, whom we passed hereabouts, floating buoyantly amid the reflections of the trees, like a feather in mid air, or a leaf which is wafted gently from its twig to the water without turning over, seemed still in their element, and to have very delicately availed themselves of the natural laws. Their floating there was a beautiful and successful experiment in natural philosophy, and it served to enoble in our eyes the art of navigation, for as birds fly and fishes swim, so these men sailed. It reminded us how much fairer and nobler all the actions of man might be, and that our life in its whole economy might be as beautiful as the fairest works of art or nature.

A Week, 48–49

You could any where run across the stream on the rocks, and its constant murmuring would quiet the passions of mankind forever.

A Week, 203

It might be seen by what tenure men held the earth. The smallest stream is *mediterranean* sea, a smaller ocean creek within the land, where men may steer by their farm bounds and cottage lights.

A Week, 238

All the world reposes in beauty to him who preserves equipoise in his life, and moves serenely on his path without secret violence; as he who sails down a stream, he has only to steer, keeping his bark in the middle, and carry it round the falls. The ripples curled away in our wake, like ringlets from the head of a child, while we steadily held on our course.

A Week, 317

While I sit here listening to the waves which ripple and break on this shore, I am absolved from all obligation to the past.

A Week, 359

The Indians say, that the river once ran both ways, one half up and the other down, but, that since the white man came, it all runs down, and now they must laboriously pole their canoes against the stream and carry them over numerous portages.

The Maine Woods, 32–33

After such a voyage, the troubled and angry waters, which once had seemed terrible and not to be trifled with, appeared tamed and subdued; they had been bearded and worried in their channels, pricked and whipped into submission with the spike-pole and paddle, gone through and through with impunity, and all their spirit and their danger taken out of them, and the most swollen and impetuous rivers seemed but playthings henceforth.

The Maine Woods, 77

The shores of the Soreal, Richelieu, or St. John's River are flat and reedy, where I had expected something more rough and mountainous for a natural boundary between two nations.

"A Yankee in Canada," *Writings* V: 8

Life in us is like the water in a river.

Walden, 332

In this lonely glen, with its brook draining the slopes, the creased ice and crystals of all hues, where the spruces and hemlocks stand up on either side, and the rush and sere wild oaks in the rivulet itself, our lives are more serene and worthy to contemplate.

"A Winter Walk," *Essays,* 59

Some months ago I went to see a panorama of the Rhine. It was like a dream of the Middle Ages. I floated down its historic stream in something more than imagination, under bridges built by the Romans, and repaired by later heroes, past cities and castles whose very names were music to my ears, and each of which was the subject of a legend. There were Ehrenbreitstein and Rolandseck and Coblentz, which I knew only in history. They were ruins that interested me chiefly. There seemed to come up from its waters and its vineclad hills and valleys a hushed music as of Crusaders departing for the Holy Land. I floated along under the spell of enchantment, as if I had been transported to an heroic age, and breathed an atmosphere of chivalry.

Soon after, I went to see a panorama of the Mississippi, and as I worked my way up the river in the light of today, and saw the steamboats wooding up, counted the rising cities, gazed on the fresh ruins of Nauvoo, beheld the Indians moving west across the stream, and, as before I had looked up the Moselle, now looked up the Ohio and the Missouri and heard the legends of Dubuque and of Wenona's Cliff, — still thinking more of the future than of the past or the present, — I saw that this was a Rhine stream of a different kind; that the foundations of castles were yet to be laid, and the famous bridges were yet to be thrown over the river; and I felt that *this was the heroic age itself,* though we know it not, for the hero is commonly the simplest and obscurest of men.

The West of which I speak is but another name for the Wild; and what I have been preparing to say is, that in Wildness is the preservation of the World.

"Walking," *Essays,* 111–12

I stood by the river today considering the forms of the elms reflected in the water. For every oak and birch too, growing on the hill top, as well as for elms and willows, there is a graceful etherial tree making down from the roots — as it were the original idea of the tree, and sometimes nature in high tides brings her mirror to its foot and makes it visible — Anxious nature sometimes reflects from pools and puddles the objects which our grovelling senses may fail to see relieved against the sky, with the pure ether for background.

15 June 1840, *Journal* 1: 127–28

I noticed a night before night before last from Fair Haven how valuable was some water by moonlight like the river & Fair Haven pond though far away — reflecting the light with a faint glimmering sheen, as in the spring of the year. The water shines with an inward light like a heaven on earth. The silent depth & serenity & majesty of water — strange that men should distinguish gold & diamonds — when these precious elements are so common. I saw a distant river by moon light making no noise, yet flowing as by day — still to the sea, like melted silver reflecting the moon light — far away it lay encircling the earth How far away it may look in the night and even from a low hill how miles away down in the valley! As far off off as Paradise and the delectable country! There is a certain glory attends on water by night. By it the heavens are related to the earth — Undistinguishable from a sky beneath you —

13 June 1851, *Journal* 3: 259–60

I hear the sound of Heywood's brook falling into Fair Haven Pond — inexpressibly refreshing to my senses — it seems to flow through my very bones. — I hear it with insatiable thirst — It allays some sandy heat in me — It affects my circulations — methinks my arteries have sympathy with it What is it I hear but the pure water falls within me in the circulation of my blood — the streams that fall into my heart? — what mists do I ever see but such as hang over — & rise from my blood — The sound of this gurgling water — running thus by night as by day — falls on all my dashes — fills all my buckets — overflows my float boards — turns all the machinery of my nature makes me a flume — a sluice way to the springs of nature — Thus I am washed thus I drink — & quench my thirst.

11 July 1851, *Journal* 3: 301

The river appears indefinitely wide — there is a mist rising from the water which increases the indefiniteness.

6 October 1851, *Journal* 4: 123

My nature may be as still as this water — but it is not so pure & its reflections are not so distinct.

11 April 1852, *Journal* 4: 438

To float thus on the silver-plated stream is like embarking on a train of thought itself. You are surrounded by water, which is full of reflections; and you see the earth at a distance, which is very agreeable to the imagination.

14 August 1854, *Journal* VI: 439

Returning, I see the red oak on R. W. E.'s shore reflected in the bright sky water. In the reflection the tree is black against the clear whitish sky, though as I see it against the opposite woods it is a warm greenish yellow. But the river sees it against the bright sky, and hence the reflection is like ink. The water tells me how it looks to it seen from below. I think that most men, as farmers, hunters, fishers, etc., walk along a river's bank, or paddle along its stream, without seeing the reflections. Their minds are not abstracted from the surface, from surfaces generally. It is only a reflecting mind that sees reflections. I am aware often that I have been occupied with shallow and commonplace thoughts, looking for something superficial, when I did not see the most glorious reflections, though exactly in the line of my vision. If the fisherman was looking at the reflection, he would not know when he had a nibble! I know from my own experience that he may cast his line right over the most elysian landscape and sky, and not *catch* the slightest notion of them. You must be in an abstract mood to see reflections however distinct. I was even startled by the sight of that reflected red oak as if it were a black water-spirit. When we are enough abstracted, the opaque earth itself reflects images to us; *i.e.,* we are imaginative, see visions, etc. Such a reflection, this inky, leafy tree, against the white sky, can only be seen at this season.

2 November 1857, *Journal* X: 156–57

What a relief and expansion of my thoughts when I come out from that inland position by the graveyard to this broad river's shore! This vista was incredible there. Suddenly I see a broad reach of blue beneath, with its curves and headlands, liberating me from the more terrene earth. What a difference it makes whether I spend my four hours' nooning between the hills by yonder roadside, or on the brink of this fair river, within a quarter of a mile of that! Here the earth is fluid to my thought, the sky is reflected from beneath, and around yonder cape is the highway to other continents. This current allies me to all the world. Be careful to sit in an elevating and inspiring place. There my thoughts were confined and trivial, and I hid myself from the gaze of travellers. Here they are expanded and elevated, and I am charmed by the beautiful river-reach. It is equal to a different season and country and creates a different mood. As you travel northward from Concord, probably the reaches of the Merrimack River, looking up or down them from the bank, will be the first inspiring sight. There is something in the scenery of a broad river equivalent to culture and civilization. Its channel conducts our thoughts as well as bodies to classic and famous ports, and allies us to all that is fair and great. I like to remember that at the end of half a day's walk I can stand on the bank of the Merrimack. It is just wide enough to interrupt the land and lead my eye and thoughts down its channel to the sea. A river is superior to a lake in its liberating influence. It has motion and indefinite length. A river touching the back of a town is like a wing, it may be unused as yet, but ready to waft it over the world. With its rapid current it is a slightly fluttering wing. River towns are winged towns.

2 July 1858, *Journal* XI: 4–5

I think that I speak impartially when I say that I have never met with a stream so suitable for boating and botanizing as the Concord, and fortunately nobody knows it. I know of reaches which a single countryseat would spoil beyond remedy, but there has not been any important change here since I can remember. The willows slumber along its shore, piled in light but low masses, even like the cumuli clouds above. We pass haymakers in every meadow, who may think that we are idlers. But Nature takes care that every nook and crevice is explored by some one. While they look after the open meadows, we farm the tract between the river's brinks and behold the shores from that side. We, too, are harvesting an annual crop with our eyes, and think you Nature is not glad to display her beauty to us?

6 August 1858, *Journal* XI: 77

NATURE IDEALIZED

How perfectly new and fresh the world is seen to be, when we behold a myriad sparkles of brilliant white sunlight on a rippled stream.

Other roads do some violence to Nature, and bring the traveller to stare at her, but the river steals into the scenery it traverses without intrusion, silently creating and adoring it, and is as free to come and go as the zephyr.

A Week, 235

The afternoon is now far advanced, and a fresh and leisurely wind is blowing over the river, making long reaches of bright ripples. The river has done its stint, and appears not to flow, but lie at its length reflecting the light, and the haze over the woods is like the inaudible panting, or rather the gentle perspiration of resting nature, rising from a myriad of pores into the attenuated atmosphere.

A Week, 320

With our heads so low in the grass, we heard the river whirling and sucking, and lapsing downward, kissing the shore as it went, sometimes rippling louder than usual, and again its mighty current making only a slight limpid trickling sound, as if our water-pail had sprung a leak, and the water were flowing into the grass by our side.

A Week, 332

We heard the sigh of the first autumnal wind, and even the water had acquired a greyer hue.

A Week, 335

This small river falls perpendicularly nearly two hundred and fifty feet at one pitch. The St. Lawrence falls only one hundred and sixty-four feet at Niagara. It is a very simple and noble fall, and leaves nothing to be desired ... It is a splendid introduction to the scenery of Quebec. Instead of an artificial fountain in its square, Quebec has this magnificent natural waterfall, to adorn one side of its harbor. Within the mouth of the chasm below, which can be entered only at ebb-tide, we have a grand view at once of Quebec and of the fall. Kalm says that the noise of the fall is sometimes heard at Quebec, about eight miles distant, and is the sign of a northeast wind.

"A Yankee in Canada," *Writings* V: 38–39

Though all the while we had grand views of the adjacent country far up and down the river, and, for the most part, when we turned about, of Quebec in the horizon behind us, and we never beheld it without new surprise and admiration; yet, throughout our walk, the Great River of Canada on our right hand was the main feature in the landscape, and this expands so rapidly below the Isle of Orleans, and creates such a breadth of level horizon above its waters in that direction, that, looking down the river as we approached the extremity of that island, the St. Lawrence seemed to be opening into the ocean, though we were still about three hundred and twenty-five miles from what can be called its mouth.

"A Yankee in Canada," *Writings* V: 49

Beyond this we by good luck fell into another path, and following this or a branch of it, at our discretion, through a forest consisting of large white pines, — the first we had seen in our walk, — we at length heard the roar of falling water, and came out at the head of the Falls of St. Anne. We had descended into a ravine or cleft in the mountain, whose walls rose still a hundred feet above us, though we were near its top, and we now stood on a very rocky shore, where the water had lately flowed a dozen feet higher, as appeared by the stones and driftwood, and large birches twisted and splintered as a farmer twists a withe. Here the river, one or two hundred feet wide, came flowing rapidly over a rocky bed out of that interesting wilderness which stretches toward Hudson's Bay and Davis's Straits. Ha-ha Bay, on the Saguenay, was about one hundred miles north of where we stood. Looking on the map, I find that the first country on the north which bears a name is that part of Rupert's Land called East Main. This river, called after the holy Anne, flowing from such a direction, here tumbled over a precipice, at present by three channels, how far down I do not know, but far enough for all our purposes, and to as good a distance as if twice as far. It matters little whether you call it one, or two, or three hundred feet; at any rate, it was a sufficient water privilege for us. I crossed the principal channel directly over the verge of the fall, where it was contracted to about fifteen feet in width, by a dead tree which had been dropped across and secured in a cleft of the opposite rock, and a smaller one a few feet higher, which served for a hand-rail. This bridge was rotten as well as small and slippery, being stripped of bark, and I was obliged to seize a moment to pass when the falling water did not surge over it, and midway, though at the expense of wet feet, I looked down probably more than a hundred feet, into the mist and foam below. This gave me the freedom of an island of precipitous rock by which I descended as by giant steps, — the rock being composed of large cubical masses, clothed with delicate close-hugging lichens of various colors, kept fresh and bright by the moisture, — till I viewed the first fall from the front, and looked down still deeper to where the second and third channels fell into a remarkable large circular basin worn in the stone. The falling water seemed to jar the very rocks, and the noise to be ever increasing. The vista down-stream was through a narrow and deep cleft in the mountain, all white suds at the bottom; but a sudden angle in this gorge prevented my seeing through to the bottom of the fall. Returning to the shore, I made my way down-stream through the forest to see how far the fall extended, and how the river came out of that adventure. It was to clamber along the side of a precipitous mountain of loose mossy rocks, covered with a damp primitive forest, and terminating at the bottom in an abrupt precipice over the stream. This was the east side of the fall. At length, after a quarter of a mile, I got down to still water, and, on looking up through the winding gorge, I could just see to the foot of the fall which I had before examined; while from the opposite side of the stream, here much contracted, rose a perpendicular wall, I will not venture to say how many hundred feet, but only that it was the highest perpendicular wall of bare rock that I ever saw. In front of me tumbled in from the summit of the cliff a tributary stream, making a beautiful cascade, which was a remarkable fall in itself, and there was a cleft in this precipice, apparently four or five feet wide, perfectly straight up and down from top to bottom, which, from its cavernous depth and darkness, appeared merely *as a black streak.*

"A Yankee in Canada," *Writings* V: 53–55

It is evident that this was the country for waterfalls; and that every stream that empties into the St. Lawrence, for some hundreds of miles, must have a great fall or cascade on it...

Falls there are a drug, and we became quite dissipated in respect to them. We had drank too much of them. Beside these which I have referred to, there are a thousand other falls on the St. Lawrence and its tributaries which I have not seen nor heard of; and above all there is one which I have heard of, called Niagara, so that I think that this river must be the most remarkable for its falls of any in the world.

"A Yankee in Canada," *Writings* V: 58–59

I saw here the most brilliant rainbow that I ever imagined. It was just across the stream below the precipice, formed on the mist which this tremendous fall produced; and I stood on a level with the keystone of its arch. It was not a few faint prismatic colors merely, but a full semicircle, only four or five rods in diameter, though as wide as usual, so intensely bright as to pain the eye, and apparently as substantial as an arch of stone. It changed its position and colors as we moved, and was the brighter because the sun shone so clearly and the mist was so thick. Evidently a picture painted on mist for the men and animals that came to the falls to look at, but for what special purpose beyond this, I know not.

"A Yankee in Canada," *Writings* V: 71

In the brooks is heard the slight grating sound of small cakes of ice, floating with various speed, full of content and promise, and where the water gurgles under a natural bridge, you may hear these hasty rafts hold conversation in an undertone. Every rill is a channel for the juices of the meadow. In the ponds the ice cracks with a merry and inspiriting din, and down the larger streams is whirled grating hoarsely, and crashing its way along, which was so lately a highway for the woodman's team and the fox, sometimes with the tracks of the skaters still fresh upon it, and the holes cut for pickerel. Town committees anxiously inspect the bridges and causeways, as if by mere eye-force to intercede with the ice and save the treasury.

"Natural History of Massachusetts," *Essays,* 18

The river swelleth more and more,
Like some sweet influence stealing o'er
The passive town; and for a while
Each tussock makes a tiny isle,

Where, on some friendly Ararat,
Resteth the weary water-rat.
No ripple shows Musketaquid,
Her very current e'en is hid,
As deepest souls do calmest rest
When thoughts are swelling in the breast,
And she that in the summer's drought
Doth make a rippling and a rout,
Sleeps from Nahshawtuck to the Cliff,
Unruffled by a single skiff.
But by a thousand distant hills
The louder roar a thousand rills,
And many a spring which now is dumb,
And many a stream with smothered hum,
Doth swifter well and faster glide,
Though buried deep beneath the tide.
Our village shows a rural Venice,
Its broad lagoons where yonder fen is;
As lovely as the Bay of Naples
Yon placid cove amid the maples;
And in my neighbor's field of corn
I recognize the Golden Horn.

Here Nature taught from year to year,
When only red men came to hear, —
Methinks 'twas in this school of art
Venice and Naples learned their part;
But still their mistress, to my mind,
Her young disciples leaves behind.
"Natural History of Massachusetts," *Essays*, 18–19

From Ball's Hill to Billerica meeting-house the river is a
noble stream of water, flowing between gentle hills and

occasional cliffs, and well wooded all the way. It can hardly be said to flow at all, but rests in the lap of the hills like a quiet lake. The boatmen call it a dead stream. For many long reaches you can see nothing to indicate that men inhabit its banks. Nature seems to hold a sabbath herself to-day, — a still warm sun on river and wood, and not breeze enough to ruffle the water. Cattle stand up to their bellies in the river, and you think Rembrandt should be here.

1 September 1839, *Journal* I: 90

The trees have come down to the bank to see the river go by. This old familiar river is renewed each instant — only the channel is the same. The water which so calmly reflects the fleeting clouds and the primeval trees I have never seen before — it may have washed some distant shore — or framed a glacier or iceberg at the north when I last stood here.

15 November 1841, *Journal* 1: 344

Water is so much more fine and sensitive an element than earth. A single boat man passing up or down unavoidably shakes the whole of a wide river, and disturbs its every reflection

19 September 1850, *Journal* 3: 120

I am accustomed to regard the smallest brook with as much interest for the time being as if it were the Orinoco or Mississippi — what is the difference I would like to know but mere size — And when a tributary rill empties in it is like the confluence of famous rivers I have read of. When I cross one on a fence I love to pause in mid-pas-

sage and look down into the water — & study its bottom
its little mystery —

16 November 1850, *Journal* 3: 140

There is something more than association at the bottom
of the excitement which the roar of a cataract produces. It
is allied to the circulation in our veins We have a waterfall
which corresponds even to Niagara somewhere within
us. It is astonishing what a rush & tumult a slight inclination will produce in a swollen brook. How it proclaims
its glee — its boisterousness — rushing headlong in its
prodigal course as if it would exhaust itself in half an
hour — how it spends itself — I would say to the orator
and poet Flow freely & *lavishly* as a brook that is full —
without stint — perchance I have stumbled upon the origin of the word lavish. It does not hesitate to tumble
down the steepest precipice & roar or tinkle as it goes, —
for fear it will exhaust its fountain. — The impetuosity of
descending waters even by the slightest inclination! It
seems to flow with ever increasing rapidity.

12 February 1851, *Journal* 3: 189

All distant landscapes — seen from hill tops are veritable
pictures — which will be found to have no actual existence to him who travels to them — "Tis distance lends
enchantment to the view." It is the bare *land*-scape without this depth of atmosphere to glass it. The distant river
reach seen in the north from the Lincoln Hill, high in the
horizon — like the ocean stream flowing round Homer's
shield — the rippling waves reflecting the light — is unlike the same seen near at hand. Heaven intervenes between me and the object — by what license do I call it
Concord River. It redeems the character of rivers to see

them thus — They were worthy then of a place on Homer's shield —

1 May 1851, Journal 3: 212–13

Returning a mist is on the river. The river is taken into the womb of nature again.

14 June 1851, Journal 3: 268

The mere surface of water was an object for the eye to linger on.

29 June 1851, Journal 3: 279

Coming out of town — willingly as usual — when I saw that reach of Charles River just above the Depot — the fair still water this cloudy evening suggesting the way to eternal peace & beauty — whence it flows — the placid lake-like fresh water so unlike the salt brine — affected me not a little — I was reminded of the way in which Wordsworth so coldly speaks of some natural visions or scenes "giving him pleasure". This is perhaps the first vision of elysium on this route from Boston.

And just then I saw an encampment of Penobscots — their wigwams appearing above the rail road fence — they too looking up the river as they sat on the ground & enjoying the scene. What can be more impressive than to look up a noble river just at evening — one perchance which you have never explored — & behold its placid waters reflecting the woods — & sky lapsing inaudibly toward the ocean — to behold as a lake — but know it as a river — tempting the beholder to explore it — & his own destiny at once.

9 July 1851, Journal 3: 297

The yellow lilies reign in the river — The painted tortoises drop off the willow stumps as you go over the bridge — The river is now so low that you can see its bottom shined on by the sun — & travellers stop to look at fishes as they go over — leaning on the rails.

16 July 1851, *Journal* 3: 309

Half an hour before sunset I was at Tupelo Cliff — when looking up from my botanizing (I had been examining the Ranunculus filiformis — the Conium Maculatum — the sium latifolium — & the obtuse galium on the muddy shore —) I saw the seal of evening on the river. There was a quiet beauty in the landscape at that hour which my senses were prepared to appreciate.

31 August 1851, *Journal* 4: 22

When I have walked all day in vain under the torrid sun — and the world has been all trivial as well field & wood as highway — then at eve the sun goes down westward — & the wind goes down with it — & the dews begin to purify the air & make it transparent and the lakes & rivers acquire a glassy stillness — reflecting the skies — the reflex of the day — I too am at the top of my condition for perceiving beauty —

31 August 1851, *Journal* 4: 23

We drink in the meadow at 2nd Division Brook — then sit awhile to watch its yellowish pebbles & the cress? in it & other weeds The ripples cover its surface like a network & are faithfully reflected on the bottom. In some places the sun reflected from ripples on a flat stone looks like a golden comb — The whole brook seems as busy as a loom — it is a woof & warp of ripples — fairy fingers are throwing the shuttle at every step — & the long waving brook is the fine product. The water is wonderfully clear.

4 September 1851, *Journal* 4: 40

As I look back up the stream from near the bridge (I suppose on the road from Potters' house to stow) I on the RR, I saw the ripples sparkling in the sun — reminding me of the sparkling icy fleets which I saw last winter — and I saw how one corresponded to the other — ice waves to water ones — the erect ice flakes were the waves stereotyped. It was the same sight — the reflection of the sun sparkling from a myriad slanting surfaces at a distance — a rippled water surface or a crystalized frozen one.

4 September 1851, *Journal* 4: 43

Lower down I see the moon in the water as bright as in the heavens — only the water bugs disturb its disk — and now I catch a faint glassy glare from the whole river surface which before was simply dark. This is set in a frame of double darkness on the east i.e. the reflected shore of woods & hills & the reality — the shadow & the substance bipartite answering to each. I see the northern lights over my shoulder to remind of the Esquimaux & that they are still my contemporaries on this globe — that they too are taking their walks on another part of the planet. — in pursuit of seals perchance.

The stars are dimly reflected in the water — The path of water-bugs in the moon's rays is like ripples of light. It is only when you stand fronting the sun or moon that you see their light reflected in the water.

7 September 1851, *Journal* 4: 57–58

What can be handsomer for a picture than our river
scenery now! Take this view from the first Conantum
Cliff. First this smoothly shorne meadow on the west side
of the stream, with all the swathes distinct — Sprinkled
with apple trees casting heavy shadows — black as ink,
such as can be seen only in this clear air. — this strong
light — one cow wandering restlessly about in it and low-
ing. — Then the blue river — scarcely darker than and not
to be distinguished from the sky — its waves driven southward, or up stream by the wind — making it appear to
flow that way bordered by willows & button bushes. —

24 September 1851, *Journal* 4: 94

The portion of the river between Bedford and Carlisle
seen from a distance in the road today as formerly has a
singularly etherial celestial, or elysian look. It is of a light
sky-blue alternating with smoother white streaks, where
the surface reflects the light differently — like a milk-pan
full of the milk of Valhalla partially skimmed more glori-
ously & heavenly fair & pure than the sky itself. It is
something more celestial than the sky above it. I never
saw any water look so celestial. I have often noticed it. I
believe I have seen this reach from the hill in the middle
of Lincoln. We have names for the rivers of hell but none
for the rivers of heaven., unless the milky way be one. It is
such a smooth & shining blue — like a panoply of sky-
blue plates — Our dark & muddy river has such a tint in
this case as I might expect Walden or White Pond to ex-
hibit if they could be seen under similar circumstances —
but Walden seen from Fair Haven is if I remember — of a
deep blue color tinged with green. Cerulian? Such water
as that river reach appears to me of quite incalculable

value, and the man who would blot that out of his prospect for a sum of money — does not otherwise than to sell heaven.

6 October 1851, Journal 4: 122

We turned down the brook at Heywood's meadow. It was worth the while to see how the water even in the marsh where the brook is almost stagnant sparkled in this atmosphere — for though warm it is remarkably clear. Water which in summer would look dark & perhaps turbid now sparkles like the lakes in November. This water is the more attractive since all around is deep snow.

25 January 1852, Journal 4: 285

Ah then the brook beyond — its rippling waters & its sunny sands. — They made me forget that it was winter — where springs oozed out of the soft bank over the dead leaves & the green sphagnum they had melted the snow or the snow had melted as it fell perchance — and the rabbits had sprinkled the mud about on the snow. The sun reflected from the sandy gravelly bottom, sometimes a bright sunny streak no bigger than your finger reflected from a ripple as from a prism — & the sunlight reflected from a hundred points of the surface of the rippling brook — enabled me to realize summer. But the dog partly spoiled the transparency of the water by running in the brook. A pup that had never seen a summer brook.

25 January 1852, Journal 4: 286

Now I see the river reach far in the north. The more distant river is ever the most etherial.

1 April 1852, Journal 4: 412

Sat awhile before sun-set on the rocks in Saw Mill Brook
— A brook need not be large to afford us pleasure by its
sands & meanderings and falls & their various accompa-
niments. It is not so much size that we want as picturesque beauty & harmony. If the sound of its fall fills
my ear it is enough. I require that the rocks over which it
falls be agreeably disposed, & prefer that they be covered
with lichens. The height & volume of the fall is of very
little importance compared with the appearance & dis-
position of the rocks over which it falls, the agreeable di-
versity of still water rapids & falls & of the surrounding
scenery. I require that the banks & neighboring hill sides
be not cut off — but excite a sense of at least graceful
wildness. One or two small evergreens, especially hemlocks standing gracefully on the brink of the rill contrasting by their green with the surrounding deciduous trees
when they have lost their leaves, & thus enlivening the
scene & betraying their attachment to the water It would
be no more pleasing to me if the stream were a mile wide
& the (trees) hemlocks 5 feet in diameter. I believe that
there is a harmony between the hemlock & the hemlock
& the water which it overhangs — not explainable. In the
first place its green is especially grateful to the eye the
greater part of the year in any locality. and in the winter
by its verdure overhanging & shading the water it con-
centrates in itself the beauty of all fluviatile trees. It loves
to stand with its foot close to the water — its roots running over the rocks of the shore — & it 2 or more on opposite sides of a brook make the makes the most beautiful
frame to a water-scape especially in deciduous woods —
where the light is somber & not too glaring. It makes the
more complete frame because its branches — particularly
in young specimens such as I am thinking of spring from

so near the ground & it makes so dense a mass of verdure. There are many larger hemlocks covering the steep
side a hill forming the bank of the assabet where they are
successively undermined by the water and they lean at
every angle over the water—some are almost horizon-
tally directed, and almost every year one falls in & is
washed away. The place is known as the "Leaning Hemlocks."

1 April 1852, *Journal* 4: 412–13

The water is dull & dark except close to the windward
shore where there is a smooth strip a rod or more in
width protected from the wind—which reflects a faint
light. When the moon reaches a clear space the water is
suddenly lit up quite across the meadows for half a mile
in length and several rods in width, while the woods beyond are thrown more into the shade or seen more in a
mass and indistinctly than before. The ripples on the
river seen in the moon-light—those between the sunken
willow lines have this form.

as if their extremities were retarded by the friction of the
banks. I noticed this afternoon—that bank below Cae-
sar's now partially flooded—higher than the neighboring meadow so that sometimes you can walk down on it a
mile dryshod with water on both sides of you. Like the
banks of the Mississippi. There always appears to be
something phosphorescent in moonlight reflected from
water.

3 April 1852, *Journal* 4: 424–25

It is refreshing to stand on the face of the Cliff—& see the water gliding over the surface of the almost perpendicular rock in a broad thin sheet—pulsing over it—It reflects the sun for half a mile like a patch of snow—As you stand close by bringing out the colors of the lichens like polishing or varnish. It is admirable regarded as a dripping fountain—

4 April 1852, *Journal* 4: 427

A river is best seen breaking through highlands—issuing from some narrow pass—It imparts a sense of power.

11 April 1852, *Journal* 4: 437

We love to see streams colored by the earth they have flown over as well as pure.

16 April 1852, *Journal* 4: 456

I think our overflowing river—far handsomer & more abounding in soft and beautiful contrasts—than a merely broad river would be—A succession of bays it is—a chain of lakes—an endlessly scolloped shore——rounding wood & field—cultivated field & wood & pasture and house are brought into ever new & unexpected positions & relations to the water. There is just stream enough for a flow of thought—that is all.—Many a foreigner who has come to this town has worked for years on its banks without discovering which way the river runs.

16 April 1852, *Journal* 4: 458

Stood by the river side early this morning. The water has been rising during the night. The sun has been shining on it half an hour. It is quite placid. The village smokes are seen against the long hill. And now I see the river also is awakening — a slight ripple beginning to appear on its surface. It wakens like the village —

Sat on the smooth river bank under Fair Haven — The sun-light in the wood across the stream. It proves a breezy afternoon. There are fresh cobwebs on the alders in the sun. The atmosphere grows somewhat misty & blue in the distance. The sun sparkle on the water is it not brighter now than it will be in summer? In this freshet & overflow — the permanent shore & shore-marks are obliterated — and the wooded point making into the water — shows no gradations — no naked stems beneath — but the pine boughs & the bushes actually rest gently on the water

There is no shore. The waters steal so gently and noiselessly over the land amid the alders & the copses — So soft so placid a shore — which would not wreck a cran-berry! The groves are simply immersed — as when you raise the water in a wine glass by dropping pins into it.

The river appears covered with an almost imperceptible blue film. The sun is not yet over the bank. What wealth in a stagnant river! There is music in every sound in the morning atmosphere. As I look up over the bay I see the reflections of the meadow woods & the Hosmer hill at a distance — the tops of the trees cut off by a slight ripple. Even the fine grasses on the near bank are distinctly re-flected. Owing to the reflections of the distant woods and hills you seem to be paddling into a vast hollow country

—doubly novel & interesting—Thus the voyageur is lured onward to fresh pastures.

16 June 1852, *Journal* 5: 103

We are favored in having two rivers—flowing into one—whose banks afford different kinds of scenery—the streams being of different characters—One a dark muddy-dead stream full of animal & vegetable life—with broad meadows—and black dwarf willows & weeds—the other *comparatively*—pebbly & swift with more abrupt banks—& narrower meadows. To the latter I go to see the ripple—& the varied bottom—with its stones & sands & shadows—to the former for the influence of its dark water resting on invisible mud—& for its reflections. It is a factory of soil-depositing sediment.

5 July 1852, *Journal* 5: 186

This redness is at first intenser as reflected in the river—as when you look into the horizon with inverted head all colors are intensified. Methinks I hear my old friend the locust in the alders. The river is perfectly smooth reflecting the golden sky & the red—for there is an unexpectedly bright & general golden or amber glow from the upper atmosphere in the W. At evening lakes & rivers become thus placid. Every dimple made by a fish or insect is betrayed as evening descends on the waters. There is not a breath of air. Now is the time to be on the water for there is no mist rising & little evening coolness or damp. At morning & at evening this precious color suffuses the sky—Evening is the reverse of the day with all its stages intensified and exaggerated.

21 July 1852, *Journal* 5: 237–38

The river is silvery as it were plated & polished smooth — with the slightest possible tinge of gold to night. How beautiful the meanders of a river thus revealed — How beautiful hills & vales — the whole surface of the earth a succession of these great cups — falling — away from dry or rocky edges to gelid green meadows & water in the midst — where night already is setting in.

27 July 1852, *Journal* 5: 262

I float slowly down from Fair Haven till I have passed the bridge. The sun 1/2 hour high has come out again just before setting with a brilliant warm light — & there is the slightest undulation discernible on the water from the boat or other cause, as it were its imitation in glass. The reflections are perfect. A bright fresh green on fields & trees now after the rain — spring-like with the sense of summer past. The reflections are the more perfect for the blackness of the water. I see the down of a thistle probably in the air descending to the water 2 or 3 rods off —, which I mistake for a man in his shirt sleeves descending a distant hill — by an ocular delusion — How fair the smooth green swells of those low grassy hills on which the sun light falls!

31 August 1852, *Journal* 5: 328

As we stand on Nawshawtuct at 5 P.M., looking over the meadows, I doubt if there is a town more adorned by its river than ours. Now the sun is low in the west, the northeasterly water is of a peculiarly ethereal light blue, more beautiful than the sky, and this broad water with innumerable bays and inlets running up into the land on either side and often divided by bridges and causeways, as if it were the very essence and richness of the heavens distilled and poured over the earth, contrasting with the clear russet land and the paler sky from which it has been subtracted,—nothing can be more elysian. Is not the blue more ethereal when the sun is at this angle?

7 April 1853, *Journal* V: 102

Climbed the wooded hill by Holden's spruce swamp and got a novel view of the river and Fair Haven Bay through the almost leafless woods. How much handsomer a river or lake such as ours, seen thus through a foreground of scattered or else partially leafless trees, though at a considerable distance this side of it, especially if the water is open, without wooded shores or isles! It is the most perfect and beautiful of all frames, which yet the sketcher is commonly careful to brush aside. I mean a pretty thick foreground, a view of the distant water through the near forest, through a thousand little vistas, as we are rushing toward the former,—that intimate mingling of wood and water which excites an expectation which the near and open view rarely realizes. We prefer that some part be concealed, which our imagination may navigate.

6 November 1853, *Journal* V: 480–81

Saw the sun reflected up from the Assabet to the hill-top, through the dispersing fog, giving to the water a peculiarly rippled, pale-golden hue,—"gilding pale streams with heavenly alchemy."

17 June 1854, *Journal* VI: 362

The beauty of the sunset is doubled by the reflection. Being on the water we have double the amount of lit and dun-colored sky above and beneath. An elm in the yellow twilight looks very rich, as if moss- or ivy-clad, and a dark-blue cloud extends into the dun-golden sky, on which there is a little fantastic cloud like a chicken walking up the point of it, with its neck outstretched. The reflected sky is more dun and richer than the real one. Take a glorious sunset sky and double it, so that it shall extend downward beneath the horizon as much as above it, blotting out the earth, and [let] the lowest half be of the deepest tint, and every beauty more than before insisted on, and you seem withal to be floating directly into it. This seems the first autumnal sunset.

7 September 1854, *Journal* VII: 19–20

Good sleighing still, with but little snow. A warm, thawing day. The river is open almost its whole length. It is a beautifully smooth mirror within an icy frame. It is well to improve such a time to walk by it. This strip of water of irregular width over the channel, between broad fields of ice, looks like a polished silver mirror, or like another surface of polished ice, and often is distinguished from the surrounding ice only by its reflections. I have rarely seen any reflections — of weeds, willows, and elms, and the houses of the village — so distinct, the stems so black and distinct; for they contrast not with a green meadow but clear white ice, to say nothing of the silvery surface of the water. Your eye slides first over a plane surface of smooth ice of one color to a water surface of silvery smoothness, like a gem set in ice, and reflecting the weeds and trees and houses and clouds with singular beauty. The reflections are particularly simple and distinct. These twigs are not referred to and confounded with a broad green meadow from which they spring, as in summer, but, instead of that dark-green ground, absorbing the light, is this abrupt white field of ice. We see so little open and smooth water at this season that I am inclined to improve such an opportunity to walk along the river, and moreover the meadows, being more or less frozen, make it more feasible than in summer.

14 December 1854, *Journal* VII: 82–83

Perhaps what most moves us in winter is some reminiscence of far-off summer. How we leap by the side of the open brooks! What beauty in the running brooks! What life! What society! The cold is merely superficial; it is summer still at the core, far, far within.

12 January 1855, *Journal* VII: 112

It [the willow *Salix lucida*] transports me in imagination to the Saskatchewan. It grows alike on the bank of the Concord and of the Mackenzie River, proving them a kindred soil. I see their broad and glossy leaves reflecting the autumn light this moment all along those rivers. Through this leaf I communicate with the Indians who roam the boundless Northwest. It tastes the same nutriment in sand of the Assabet and its water as in that of the Saskatchewan and Jasper Lake, suggesting that a short time ago the shores of this river were as wild as the shores of those.

2 September 1856, *Journal* IX: 56

Looking at the reflection of the bank by the Hemlocks, the reflected sun dazzles me, and I approach nearer to the bank in order to shut it out (of course it disappears sooner in the reflection than the substance, because every head is raised above the level of the water), and I see in the reflection the fine, slender grasses on the sharp or well-defined edge of the bank all glowing with silvery light, a singularly silvery light to be seen in the water [?], and whose substance I cannot see to advantage with my head thus high, since the sun is in the way.

11 October 1857, *Journal* X: 86

That bright and warm reflection of sunlight from the insignificant edging of stubble was remarkable. I was coming down-stream over the meadows, on the ice, within four or five rods of the eastern shore. The sun on my left was about a quarter of an hour above the horizon. The ice was soft and sodden, of a dull lead-color, quite dark and reflecting no light as I looked eastward, but my eyes caught by accident a singular sunny brightness reflected from the narrow border of stubble only three or four inches high (and as many feet wide perhaps) which rose along the edge of the ice at the foot of the hill. It was not a mere brightening of the bleached stubble, but the warm and yellow light of the sun, which, it appeared, it was peculiarly fitted to reflect. It was that amber light from the west which we sometimes witness after a storm, concentrated on this stubble, for the hill beyond was merely a dark russet spotted with snow. All the yellow rays seemed to be reflected by this insignificant stubble alone, and when I looked more generally a little above it, seeing it with the under part of my eye, it appeared yet more truly and more bright; the reflected light made its due impression on my eye, separated from the proper color of the stubble, and it glowed almost like a low, steady, and serene fire. It was precisely as if the sunlight had mechanically slid over the ice, and lodged against the stubble. It will be enough to say of something warmly and sunnily bright that it glowed like lit stubble. It was remarkable that, looking eastward, this was the only evidence of the light in the west.

4 January 1858, *Journal* X: 236–37

In the reflection the button-bushes and their balls appear against the sky, though the substance is seen against the meadow or distant woods and hills; *i.e.,* they appear in the reflection as they would if viewed from that point on the surface from which they are reflected to my eye, so that it is as if I had another eye placed there to see for me. Hence, too, we are struck by the prevalence of sky or light in the reflection, and at twilight dream that the light has gone down into the bosom of the waters; for in the reflection the sky comes up to the very shore or edge and appears to extend under it, while, the substance being seen from a more elevated point, the actual horizon is perhaps many miles distant over the fields and hills. In the reflection you have an infinite number of eyes to see for you and report the aspect of things each from its point of view. The statue in the meadow which actually is seen obscurely against the meadow, in the reflection appears dark and distinct against the sky.

16 October 1858, *Journal* XI: 213–14

There are many crisped but colored leaves resting on the smooth surface of the Assabet, which for the most part is not stirred by a breath; but in some places, where the middle is rippled by a slight breeze, no leaves are seen, while the broad and perfectly smooth portions next the shore will be covered with them, as if by a current they were prevented from falling on the other parts. These leaves are chiefly of the red maple, with some white maple, etc. To be sure, they hardly begin to conceal the river, unless in some quiet coves, yet they remind me of ditches in swamps, whose surfaces are often quite concealed by leaves now. The waves made by my boat cause them to rustle, and both by sounds and sights I am reminded that I am in the very midst of the fall.

Methinks the reflections are never purer and more distinct than now at the season of the fall of the leaf, just before the cool twilight has come, when the air has a finer grain. Just as our mental reflections are more distinct at this season of the year, when the evenings grow cool and lengthen and our winter evenings with their brighter fires may be said to begin. And painted ducks, too, often come and sail or float amid the painted leaves.

17 October 1858, *Journal* XI: 215–16

One reason why I associate perfect reflections from still water with this and a later season may be that now, by the fall of the leaves, so much more light is let in to the water. The river reflects more light, therefore, in this twilight of the year, as it were an afterglow.

17 October 1858, *Journal* XI: 217

The green of the ice and water begins to be visible about half an hour before sunset. Is it produced by the reflected blue of the sky mingling with the yellow or pink of the setting sun?

20 January 1859, *Journal* XI: 414

What a singular element is this water!

20 January 1859, *Journal* XI: 414

At Corner Spring Brook the water reaches up to the crossing and stands over the ice there, the brook being open and some space on each side of it. When I look, from forty or fifty rods off, at the yellowish water covering the ice about a foot here, it is decidedly purple (though, when close by and looking down on it, it is yellowish merely), while the water of the brook-channel and a rod on each side of it, where there is no ice beneath, is a beautiful very dark blue. These colors are very distinct, the line of separation being the edge of the ice on the bottom, and this apparent juxtaposition of different kinds of water is a very singular and pleasing sight. You see a light-purple flood, about the color of a red grape, and a broad channel of dark-purple water, as dark as a common blue-purple grape, sharply distinct across its middle.

9 March 1859, *Journal* XII: 29

Rivers, too, like the walker, unbutton their icy coats, and we see the dark bosoms of their channels in the midst of the ice. Again, in pools of melted snow, or where the river has risen, I look into clear, placid water, and see the russet grassy bottom in the sun.

10 March 1859, *Journal* XII: 32

Look up or down the open channel now, so smooth, like a hibernating animal that has ventured to come out to the mouth of its burrow. One way, perhaps, it is like melted silver alloyed with copper. It goes nibbling off the edge of the thick ice on each side. Here and there I see a musquash sitting in the sun on the edge of the ice, eating a clam, and the clamshells it has left are strewn along the edge. Ever and anon he drops into the liquid mirror, and soon reappears with another clam. This clear, placid, silvery water is evidently a phenomenon of spring. Winter could not show us this.

10 March 1859, *Journal* XII: 33

How perfectly new and fresh the world is seen to be, when we behold a myriad sparkles of brilliant white sunlight on a rippled stream! So remote from dust and decay, more bright than the flash of an eye.

24 May 1860, *Journal* XIII: 311

Lakes and Ponds

NATURE IDOLIZED
A lake is the landscape's most beautiful and expressive feature. It is earth's eye; looking into which the beholder measures the depth of his own nature.

This small lake was of most value as a neighbor in the intervals of a gentle rain storm in August, when, both air and water being perfectly still, but the sky overcast, mid-afternoon had all the serenity of evening, and the wood-thrush sang around, and was heard from shore to shore. A lake like this is never smoother than at such a time; and the clear portion of the air above it being shallow and darkened by clouds, the water, full of light and reflections, becomes a lower heaven itself so much the more important.

Walden, 86

We have one other pond just like this, White Pond in Nine Acre Corner, about two and a half miles westerly; but, though I am acquainted with most of the ponds within a dozen miles of this centre, I do not know a third of this pure and well-like character. Successive nations perchance have drank at, admired, and fathomed it, and passed away, and still its water is green and pellucid as ever. Not an intermitting spring! Perhaps on that spring morning when Adam and Eve were driven out of Eden Walden Pond was already in existence, and even then breaking up in a gentle spring rain accompanied with mist and a southerly wind, and covered with myriads of ducks and geese, which had not heard of the fall, when still such pure lakes sufficed them. Even then it had commenced to rise and fall, and had clarified its waters and colored them of the hue they now wear, and obtained a patent of heaven to be the only Walden Pond in the world and distiller of celestial dews. Who knows in how many unremembered nations' literatures this has been the Castalian Fountain? or what nymphs presided over it in the Golden Age? It is a gem of the first water which Concord wears in her coronet.

Walden, 179

A lake is the landscape's most beautiful and expressive feature. It is earth's eye; looking into which the beholder measures the depth of his own nature. The fluviatile trees next the shore are the slender eyelashes which fringe it, and the wooded hills and cliffs around are its overhanging brows.

Walden, 186

> It is no dream of mine,
> To ornament a line;
> I cannot come nearer to God and Heaven
> Than I live to Walden even.
> I am its stony shore,

And the breeze that passes o'er;
In the hollow of my hand
Are its water and its sand,
And its deepest resort
Lies high in my thought.

Walden, 193

Goose Pond, of small extent, is on my way to Flints'; Fair-Haven, an expansion of Concord River, said to contain some seventy acres, is a mile south-west; and White Pond, of about forty acres, is a mile and a half beyond Fair-Haven. This is my lake country. These, with Concord River, are my water privileges; and night and day, year in year out, they grind such grist as I carry to them.

Walden, 197

White Pond and Walden are great crystals on the surface of the earth, Lakes of Light. If they were permanently congealed, and small enough to be clutched, they would, perchance, be carried off by slaves, like precious stones, to adorn the heads of emperors; but being liquid, and ample, and secured to us and our successors forever, we disregard them, and run after the diamond of Kohinoor. They are too pure to have a market value; they contain no muck. How much more beautiful than our lives, how much more transparent than our characters, are they!

Walden, 199

What I have observed of the pond is no less true in ethics. It is the law of average. Such a rule of the two diameters not only guides us toward the sun in the system and the heart in man, but draw lines through the length and breadth of the aggregate of a man's particular daily behaviors and waves of life into his coves and inlets, and where they intersect will be the height or depth of his character. Perhaps we need only to know how his shores trend and his adjacent country or circumstances, to infer his depth and concealed bottom. If he is surrounded by mountainous circumstances, an Achillean shore, whose peaks overshadow and are reflected in his bosom, they suggest a corresponding depth in him. But a low and smooth shore proves him shallow on that side. In our bodies, a bold projecting brow falls off to and indicates a corresponding depth of thought. Also there is a bar across the entrance of our every cove, or particular incli-nation; each is our harbor for a season, in which we are detained and partially land-locked. These inclinations are not whimsical usually, but their form, size, and direc-tion are determined by the promontories of the shore, the ancient axes of elevation. When this bar is gradually in-creased by storms, tides, or currents, or there is subsi-dence of the waters, so that it reaches to the surface, that which was at first but an inclination in the shore in which a thought was harbored becomes an individual lake, cut off from the ocean, herein the thought secures its own conditions, changes, perhaps, from salt to fresh, becomes a sweet sea, dead sea, or a marsh. At the advent of each in-dividual into this life, may we not suppose that such a bar has risen to the surface somewhere? It is true, we are such poor navigators that our thoughts, for the most part, stand off and on upon a harborless coast, are conversant only with the bights of the bays of poesy, or steer for the public ports of entry, and go into the dry docks of sci-ence, where they merely refit for this world, and no nat-ural currents concur to individualize them.

Walden, 291–92

Thus it appears that the sweltering inhabitants of Charleston and New Orleans, of Madras and Bombay and Calcutta, drink at my well. In the morning I bathe my intellect in the stupendous and cosmogonal philosophy of the Bhagvat Geeta, since whose composition years of the gods have elapsed, and in comparison with which our modern world and its literature seem puny and trivial; and I doubt if that philosophy is not to be referred to a previous state of existence, so remote is its sublimity from our conceptions. I lay down the book and go to my well for water, and lo! there I meet the servant of the Brahmin, priest of Brahma and Vishnu and Indra, who still sits in his temple on the Ganges reading the Vedas, or dwells at the root of a tree with his crust and water jug. I meet his servant come to draw water for his master, and our buckets as it were grate together in the same well. The pure Walden water is mingled with the sacred water of the Ganges. With favoring winds it is wafted past the site of the fabulous islands of Atlantis and the Hesperides, makes the periplus of Hanno, and floating by Ternate and Tidore and the mouth of the Persian Gulf, melts in the tropic gales of the Indian seas, and is landed in ports of which Alexander only heard the names.

Walden, 297–98

I do not suppose that I have attained to obscurity, but I should be proud if no more fatal fault were found with my pages on this score than was found with the Walden ice. Southern customers objected to its blue color, which is the evidence of its purity, as if it were muddy, and preferred the Cambridge ice, which is white, but tastes of

weeds. The purity men love is like the mists which en-
velop the earth, and not like the azure ether beyond.

Walden, 325

Near the lake, which we were approaching with as much
expectation as if it had been a university, — for it is not often that the stream of our life opens into such expan-
sions, — were islands, and a low and meadowy shore
with scattered trees.

The Maine Woods, 122–23

It is an agreeable change to cross a lake, after you have
been shut up in the woods, not only on account of the
greater expanse of water, but also of sky. It is one of the
surprises which Nature has in store for the traveller in the
forest. To look down, in this case, over eighteen miles of
water, was liberating and civilizing even. . . . The lakes
also reveal the mountains, and give ample scope and
range to our thought.

The Maine Woods, 197–98

While I bask in the sun on the shores of Walden pond, by
this heat and this rustle I am absolved from all obligation
to the past — The council of nations may reconsider their
votes — the grating of a pebble annuls them.

22 March 1840, *Journal* 1: 120

The waves lapse with such a melody on the shore as
shows that they have long been at one with nature.
Theirs is as perfect play as if the heavens and earth were
not — they meet with a sweet difference and indepen-
dently — as old play-fellows. Nothing do they lack more

than the world — the ripple is proud to be a ripple and balances the sea.

7–10 March 1841, *Journal* 1: 281

I see three little lakes between the hills near its edge — reflecting the sun's rays. — The light glimmers as on the water in a tumbler. So far off do the laws of reflection hold. I seem to see the ribs of the creature. This is the aspect of their day its outside — their heaven above their heads, towards which they breathe their prayers. So much is between me and them. It is noon there perchance and ships are at anchor in the havens or sailing on the seas. and there is a din in the streets — and in this light or that shade some leisurely soul contemplates.

2 June 1841, *Journal* 1: 312–13

I seem to discern the very form of the wind when blowing over the hills it falls in broad flakes upon the surface of the pond — This subtle element obeying the same law with the least subtle — As it falls it spreads itself like a mass of lead dropped upon an anvil — I cannot help being encouraged by this blithe activity in the elements — in these degenerate days of men. Who hears the rippling of the rivers will not utterly despair of anything.

The wind in the wood yonder sounds like an incessant waterfall — the water dashing and roaring among rocks.

12 November 1841, *Journal* 1: 342

I want to go soon and live away by the pond where I shall hear only the wind whispering among the reeds — It will be success if I shall have left myself behind, But my friends ask what I will do when I get there? Will it not be employment enough to watch the progress of the seasons?

15 March 1842, *Journal* 1: 347

Nature is constantly original and inventing new patterns, like a mechanic in his shop. When the overhanging pine drops into the water, by the action of the sun, and the wind rubbing it on the shore, its boughs are worn white and smooth and assume fantastic forms, as if turned by a lathe. All things, indeed, are subjected to a rotary motion, either gradual and partial or rapid and complete, from the planet and [solar] system to the simplest shellfish and pebbles on the beach; as if all beauty resulted from an object turning on its own axis, or others turning about it. It establishes a new centre in the universe. As all curves have reference to their centres or foci, so all beauty of character has reference to the soul, and is a graceful gesture of recognition or waving of the body toward it.

15 March 1842, *Journal* I: 332

A field of water betrays the spirit that is in the air. It has new life and motion. It is intermediate between land and sky. On land, only the grass and trees wave, but the water itself is *rippled* by the wind. I see the breeze dash across it in streaks and flakes of light. It is somewhat singular that we should *look down* on the surface of the water. We shall look down on the surface of air next, and mark where a still subtler spirit sweeps over *it*.

16 July 1850, *Journal* II: 57

I am made to love the pond & the meadow as the wind is made to ripple the water.

21 November 1850, *Journal* 3: 148

To be calm to be serene — there is the calmness of the lake when there is not a breath of wind — there is the calmness of a stagnant ditch. So is it with us. Sometimes we are clarified & calmed healthily as we never were before in our lives — not by an opiate — but by some unconscious obedience to the all-just laws — so that we become like a still lake of purest crystal and without an effort our depths are revealed to ourselves All the world goes by us & is reflected in our deeps. Such clarity! Obtained by such pure means! by simple living — by honesty of purpose — we live & rejoice.

22 June 1851, *Journal* 3: 274–75

What unanimity between the water & the sky — one only a little denser element than the other. The grossest part of heaven — Think of a mirror on so large a scale! Standing on distant hills you see the heavens reflected the evening sky in some low lake or river in the valley — as perfectly as in any mirror they could be — Does it not prove how intimate heaven is with earth?

31 August 1851, *Journal* 4: 25

I love to gaze at the low island in the Pond — at any island or inaccesible [*sic*] land. The isle at which you look always seems fairer than the main-land on which you stand.

12 September 1851, *Journal* 4: 79

What if all the ponds were shallow! — would it not react on the minds of men? If there were no physical deeps. I thank God that he made this pond deep & pure — for a symbol.

26 January 1852, *Journal* 4: 291

As I stand there, I see some dark ripples already drop and sweep over the surface of the pond, as they will ere long over Ripple Lake and other pools in the wood. No sooner has the ice of Walden melted than the wind begins to play in dark ripples over the surface of the virgin water. It is affecting to see Nature so tender, however old, and wearing none of the wrinkles of age. Ice dissolved is the next moment as perfect water as if it had been melted a million years. To see that which was lately so hard and immovable now so soft and impressible! What if our moods could dissolve thus completely? It is like a flush of life in a cheek that was dead. It seems as if it must rejoice in its own newly acquired fluidity, as it affects the beholder with joy. Often the March winds have no chance to ripple its face at all.

14 March 1860, *Journal* XIII, 191

NATURE IDEALIZED

I think it important to have water, because it multiplies the heavens.

For the first week, whenever I looked out on the pond it impressed me like a tarn high up on the side of a mountain, its bottom far above the surface of other lakes, and, as the sun arose, I saw it throwing off its nightly clothing of mist, and here and there, by degrees, its soft ripples or its smooth reflecting surface was revealed, while the mists, like ghosts, were stealthily withdrawing in every direction into the woods, as at the breaking up of some nocturnal conventicle. The very dew seemed to hang upon the trees later into the day than usual, as on the sides of mountains.

Walden, 86

It is well to have some water in your neighborhood, to give buoyancy to and float the earth. One value even of the smallest well is, that when you look into it you see that earth is not continent but insular. This is as important as that it keeps butter cool. When I looked across the pond from this peak toward the Sudbury meadows, which in time of flood I distinguished elevated perhaps by a mirage in their seething valley, like a coin in a basin, all the earth beyond the pond appeared like a thin crust insulated and floated even by this small sheet of intervening water, and I was reminded that this on which I dwelt was but *dry land*.

Walden, 87

I also heard the whooping of the ice in the pond, my great bed-fellow in that part of Concord, as if it were restless in its bed and would fain turn over, were troubled with flatulency and bad dreams.

Walden, 272

The shore is irregular enough not to be monotonous. I have in my mind's eye the western indented with deep bays, the bolder northern, and the beautifully scolloped southern shore, where successive capes overlap each other and suggest unexplored coves between. The forest has never so good a setting, nor is so distinctly beautiful, as when seen from the middle of a small lake amid hills which rise from the water's edge; for the water in which it is reflected not only makes the best foreground in such a case, but, with its winding shore, the most natural and agreeable boundary to it. There is no rawness nor imperfection in its edge there, as where the axe has cleared a part, or a cultivated field abuts on it. The trees have ample room to expand on the water side, and each sends forth its most vigorous branch in that direction. There Nature has woven a natural selvage, and the eye rises by just gradations from the low shrubs of the shore to the highest trees. There are few traces of man's hand to be seen. The water laves the shore as it did a thousand years ago.

Walden, 185–86

Standing on the smooth sandy beach at the east end of the pond, in a calm September afternoon, when a slight haze makes the opposite shore line indistinct, I have seen whence came the expression, "the glassy surface of a lake." When you invert your head, it looks like a thread of finest gossamer stretched across the valley, and gleaming against the distant pine woods, separating one stratum of the atmosphere from another. You would think that you could walk dry under it to the opposite hills, and that the swallows which skim over might perch on it. Indeed, they sometimes dive below the line, as it were by mistake, and are undeceived. As you look over the pond westward you are obliged to employ both your hands to defend your eyes against the reflected as well as the true sun, for they are equally bright; and if, between the two, you survey its surface critically, it is literally as smooth as glass, except where the skater insects, at equal intervals scattered over its whole extent, by their motions in the sun produce the finest imaginable sparkle on it, or, perchance, a duck plumes itself, or, as I have said, a swallow skims so low as to touch it. It may be that in the distance a fish describes an arc of three or four feet in the air, and there is one bright flash where it emerges, and another where it strikes the water; sometimes the whole silvery arc is revealed; or here and there, perhaps, is a thistle-down floating on its surface, which the fishes dart at and so dimple it again. It is like molten glass cooled but not congealed, and the few motes in it are pure and beautiful like the imperfections in glass. You may often detect a yet smoother and darker water, separated from the rest as if by an invisible cobweb loom of the water nymphs, resting on it. From a hill-top you can see a fish leap in almost any part; for not a pickerel or shiner picks an insect from this smooth surface but it manifestly disturbs the equilibrium of the whole lake. It is wonderful with what elaborateness this simple fact is advertised, — this piscine murder will out, — and from half a dozen rods in diameter. You can even detect a water-bug *(Gyrinus)* ceaselessly progressing over the smooth surface a quarter of a mile off; for they furrow the water slightly, making a conspicuous ripple bounded by two diverging lines, but the skaters glide over it without rippling it perceptibly. When the surface is considerably agitated there are no skaters nor water-bugs on it, but apparently, in calm days, they leave their havens and adventurously glide forth from the shore by short impulses till they completely cover it. It is a soothing employment, on one of those fine days in the fall when all the warmth of the sun is fully appreciated, to sit on a stump on such a height as this, overlooking the pond, and study the dimpling circles which are incessantly inscribed on its otherwise invisible surface amid the reflected skies and trees. Over this great expanse there is no disturbance but it is thus at once gently smoothed away and assuaged, as, when a vase of water is jarred, the trembling circles seek the shore and all is smooth again. Not a fish can leap or an insect fall on the pond but it is thus reported in circling dimples, in lines of beauty, as it were the constant welling up of its fountain, the gentle pulsing of its life, the heaving of its breast. The thrills of joy and thrills of pain are undistinguishable. How peaceful the phenomena of the lake! Again the works of man shine as in the spring. Ay, every leaf and twig and stone and cobweb sparkles now at mid-afternoon as when covered with dew in a spring morning. Every motion of an oar or an insect produces a flash of light; and if an oar falls, how sweet the echo!

Walden, 186–88

In such a day, in September or October, Walden is a perfect forest mirror, set round with stones as precious to my eye as if fewer or rarer. Nothing so fair, so pure, and at the same time so large, as a lake, perchance, lies on the surface of the earth. Sky water. It needs no fence. Nations come and go without defiling it. It is a mirror which no stone can crack, whose quicksilver will never wear off, whose gilding Nature continually repairs; no storms, no dust, can dim its surface ever fresh; — a mirror in which all impurity presented to it sinks, swept and dusted by the sun's hazy brush, — this the light dust-cloth, — which retains no breath that is breathed on it, but sends its own to float as clouds high above its surface, and be reflected in its bosom still.

Walden, 188

A field of water betrays the spirit that is in the air. It is continually receiving new life and motion from above. It is intermediate in its nature between land and sky. On land only the grass and trees wave, but the water itself is rippled by the wind. I see where the breeze dashes across it by the streaks or flakes of light. It is remarkable that we can look down on its surface. We shall, perhaps, look down thus on the surface of air at length, and mark where a still subtler spirit sweeps over it.

Walden, 188–89

Walden is melting apace. There is a canal two rods wide along the northerly and westerly sides, and wider still at the east end. A great field of ice has cracked off from the main body. I hear a song-sparrow singing from the bushes on the shore, — *olit, olit, olit,* — *chip, chip, chip, che char,* — *che wiss, wiss, wiss.* He too is helping to crack it. How handsome the great sweeping curves in the edge of the ice, answering somewhat to those of the shore, but more regular! It is unusually hard, owing to the recent severe but transient cold, and all watered or waved like a palace floor. But the wind slides eastward over its opaque surface in vain, till it reaches the living surface beyond. It is glorious to behold this ribbon of water sparkling in the sun, the bare face of the pond full of glee and youth, as if it spoke the joy of the fishes within it, and of the sands on its shore, — a silvery sheen as from the scales of a *leuciscus,* as it were all one active fish. Such is the contrast between winter and spring. Walden was dead and is alive again.

Walden, 311

Thus aroused, I too brought fresh fuel to the fire, and then rambled along the sandy shore in the moonlight, hoping to meet a moose come down to drink, or else a wolf. The little rill tinkled the louder, and peopled all the wilderness for me; and the glassy smoothness of the sleeping lake, laving the shores of a new world, with the dark, fantastic rocks rising here and there from its surface, made a scene not easily described. It has left such an impression of stern yet gentle wildness on my memory as will not soon be effaced.

The Maine Woods, 40

The forest looked like a firm grass sward, and the effect of these lakes in its midst has been well compared by one who has since visited this same spot, to that of a "mirror broken into a thousand fragments, and wildly scattered over the grass, reflecting the full blaze of the sun."

The Maine Woods, 66

The lakes are something which you are unprepared for: they lie up so high exposed to the light, and the forest is diminished to a fine fringe on their edges, with here and there a blue mountain, like amethyst jewels set around some jewel of the first water, — so anterior, so superior to all the changes that are to take place on their shores, even now civil and refined, and fair, as they can never be.

The Maine Woods, 80

It is remarkable how little these important gates to a lake are blazoned. There is no triumphal arch over the modest inlet or outlet, but at some undistinguished point it trickles in or out through the uninterrupted forest, almost as through a sponge.

The Maine Woods, 227–28

As you approach Lake Champlain you begin to see the New York mountains. The first view of the lake at Vergennes is impressive, but rather from association than from any peculiarity in the scenery. It lies there so small (not appearing in that proportion to the width of the State that it does on the map), but beautifully quiet, like a picture of the Lake of Lucerne on a music box, where you trace the name of Lucerne among the foliage; far more ideal than ever it looked on the map. It does not say, "Here I am, Lake Champlain," as the conductor might for it, but having studied the geography thirty years, you crossed over a hill one afternoon and beheld it. But it is only a glimpse that you get here. At Burlington you rush to a wharf and go on board a steamboat, two hundred and thirty-two miles from Boston. We left Concord at twenty minutes before eight in the morning, and were in Burlington about six at night, but too late to see the lake. We got our first fair view of the lake at dawn, just before reaching Plattsburg, and saw blue ranges of mountains on either hand, in New York and in Vermont, the former especially grand. A few white schooners, like gulls, were seen in the distance, for it is not waste and solitary like a lake in Tartary; but it was such a view as leaves not much to be said; indeed, I have postponed Lake Champlain to another day.

"A Yankee in Canada," *Writings* V: 6–7

And now we descend again, to the brink of this woodland lake, which lies in a hollow of the hills, as if it were their expressed juice, and that of the leaves which are annually steeped in it. Without outlet or inlet to the eye, it has still its history, in the lapse of the waves, in the rounded pebbles on its shore, and in the pines which grow down to its brink. It has not been idle, though sedentary, but, like Abu Musa, teaches that "sitting still at home is the heavenly way; the going out is the way of the world." Yet in its evaporation it travels as far as any. In summer it is the earth's liquid eye, a mirror in the breast of nature. The sins of the wood are washed out in it. See how the woods form an amphitheatre about it, and it is an arena for all the genialness of nature. All trees direct the traveler to its brink, all paths seek it out, birds fly to it, quadrupeds flee to it, and the very ground inclines toward it. It is nature's saloon, where she has sat down to her toilet. Consider her silent economy and tidiness; how the sun comes with his evaporation to sweep the dust from its surface each morning, and a fresh surface is constantly welling up; and annually, after whatever impurities have accumulated herein, its liquid transparency appears again in the spring. In summer a hushed music seems to sweep across its surface. But now a plain sheet of snow conceals it from our eyes, except where the wind has swept the ice bare, and the sere leaves are gliding from side to side, tacking and veering on their tiny voyages. Here is one just keeled up against a pebble on shore, a dry beech leaf, rocking still, as if it would start again. A skillful engineer, methinks, might project its course since it fell from the parent stem. Here are all the elements for such a calculation. Its present position, the direction of the wind, the level of the pond, and how much more is given. In its scarred edges and veins is its log rolled up.

We fancy ourselves in the interior of a larger house. The surface of the pond is our deal table or sanded floor, and the woods rise abruptly from its edge, like the walls of a cottage. The lines set to catch pickerel through the ice look like a larger culinary preparation, and the men stand about on the white ground like pieces of forest furniture. The actions of these men, at the distance of half a mile over the ice and snow, impress us as when we read the exploits of Alexander in history. They seem not unworthy of the scenery, and as momentous as the conquest of kingdoms.

"A Winter Walk," *Essays,* 62–63

Your account excites in me a desire to see the Middleboro Ponds, of which I had already heard somewhat; as also of some very beautiful ponds on the Cape, in Harwich I think, near which I once passed.

Letter to Daniel Ricketson, 1 October 1854, *Correspondence*

> I know the world where land and water meet,
> By yonder hill abutting on the main,
> One while I hear the waves incessant beat,
> Then turning round survey the land again.

10 January 1840, *Journal* 1: 100

One afternoon in the fall Nov 21st I saw Fair Haven Pond with its island & meadow between the island & the shore, a strip of perfectly smooth water in the lee of the island & two hawks sailing over it—(and something more I saw which cannot easily be described which made me say to myself that it the landscape could not be improved.) I did not see how it could be improved. Yet I do not know what these things can be; (for) I begin to see such objects only when I leave off understanding them—

and afterwards remember that I did not appreciate them before. But I get no further than this. How adapted these forms & colors to our eyes, a meadow & its islands. What are these things? Yet the hawks & the ducks keep so aloof, & nature is so reserved! We are made to love the river & the meadow as the wind (is made) to ripple the water

14 February 1851, *Journal* 3: 192–93

I had in my mind's eye a silent grey tarn which I had seen the summer before? high up on the side of a *mt* Bald Mt where the half dead spruce trees stood far in the water draped with wreathy mist as with esnea moss — made of dews — where the Mt spirit bathed. Whose bottom was high above the surface of other lakes Spruces whose dead limbs were more in harmony with the mists which draped them.

1 May 1851, *Journal* 3: 213

As I approached the pond down Hubbard's path (after coming out of the woods into a warmer air) I saw the shimmering of the moon on its surface — and in the near now flooded cove the water-bugs darting circling about made streaks or curves of light. The moon's inverted pyramid of shimmering light commenced about 20 rods off — like so much micaceous sand — But I was startled to see midway in the dark water a bright flame like more than phosphorescent light crowning the crests of the wavelets which at first I mistook for fire flies & and thought even of cucullos — It had the appearance of a pure smokeless flame $^{1}/_{2}$ dozen inches long issuing from the water & bending flickeringly along its surface — I thought of St

Elmo's lights & the like—but coming near to the shore of the pond itself—these flames increased & I saw that it was so many broken reflections of the moon's disk, though one would have said they were of an intenser light than the moon herself—from contrast with the surrounding water they were—Standing up close to the shore & nearer the rippled surface I saw the reflections of the moon sliding down the watery concave like so many lustrous burnished coins poured from a bag—with inexhaustible lavishness—& the lambent flames on the surface were much multiplied seeming to slide along a few inches with each wave before they were extinguished—& I saw how farther & farther off they gradually merged in the general sheen which in fact was made up of a myriad little mirrors reflecting the disk of the moon—with equal brightness to an eye rightly placed. The pyramid or sheaf of light which we see springing from near where we stand only—in fact is the outline of that portion of the shimmering surface which an eye takes in—to myriad eyes suitably placed, the whole surface of the pond would be seen to shimmer, or rather it would be seen as the waves turned up their mirrors to be covered with those bright flame like reflections of the moon's disk like a myriad candles every where issuing from the waves—i.e. if there were as many eyes as angles presented by the waves—and these reflections are dispersed in all directions into the atmosphere flooding it with light—No wonder that water reveals itself so far by night—even further in many states of the atmosphere than by day.

13 June 1851, *Journal* 3: 262–63

I walked by moon last night & saw and saw its disk reflected in Walden Pond—the broken disk, now here now

there, a pure & memorable flame unearthly bright — like
a cucullo of a water-bug. — Ah! but that first faint tinge of
moonlight on the gap! — a silvery light from the east before day had departed in the west.

6 July 1851, *Journal* 3: 285–86

The distant lamps in the farm house look like fires. The
trees & clouds are seen at a distance reflected in the river
as by day. I see Fair Haven Pond from the Cliffs — as it
were through a slight mist — it is the wildest scenery
imaginable — a Lake of the woods.

5 August 1851, *Journal* 3: 355

Moonlight on Fair Haven Pond seen from the Cliffs. A
sheeny lake in the midst of a boundless forest — The
windy surf sounding freshly & wildly in the single pine
behind you — The silence of hushed wolves in the
wilderness & as you fancy moose looking off from the
shore of the lake. The stars of poetry & history — & unexplored nature looking down on the scene. This is my
world now — with a dull whitish mark curving northward
through the forest marking the outlet to the lake. Fair
Haven by moonlight lies there like a lake in the Maine
Wilderness in the midst of a primitive forest untrodden
by man. This light & this hour takes the civilization all
out of the landscape —

5 September 1851, *Journal* 4: 47

From this point & at this height I do not perceive any
bright or yellowish light on Fair Haven — but an oily &
glass like smoothness on its southwestern bay — through
a very slight mistiness. Two or three pines appear to
stand in the moon lit air on this side of the pond — while

the Enlightened portion of the water is bounded by the heavy reflection of the wood on the east It was so soft & velvety a light as contained a thousand placid days sweetly put to rest in the bosom of the water. So looked the north Twin Lake in the Maine woods. It reminds me of placid lakes in the mid-noon of Ind. Summer days — but yet more placid & civilized — suggesting a higher cultivation — which aeons of summer days have gone to make. Like a summer day seen far away. All the effects of sunlight — with a softer tone — and all this stillness of the water & the air superadded — & the witchery of the hour. What gods are they that require so fair a vase of gleaming water to their prospect in the midst of the wild woods by night? Else why this beauty allotted to night — a gem to sparkle in the zone of night. They are strange gods now out — methinks their names are not in any mythology — I can faintly trace its zigzag border of sheeny pads even here. If such is there to be seen in re- motest wildernesses — does it not suggest its own nymphs & wood Gods to enjoy it? As When at middle of the placcid noon in Ind summer days all the surface of a lake is as one cobweb — gleaming in the sun which heaves gently to the passing zephyr — There was the lake — its glassy surface just distinguishable — its sheeny shore of pads — with a few pines bathed in light on its hither shore just as in mid of a november day — except that this was the chaster light of the moon — the cooler — temperature of the night and these were the deep shades of night that fenced it round & imbosomed. It tells of a far away long passed civilization of an antiquity superior to time — unappreciable by time.

7 September 1851, *Journal* 4: 58–59

From the Hill on the S side of the Pond — the forests
have a singularly rounded & bowery look clothing the
hills quite down to the water's edge & leaving no shore;
the Ponds are like drops of dew amid and partly covering
the leaves. So the great globe is luxuriously crowded
without margin.

22 September 1851, Journal 4: 91

I am surprised to find Flints Pond frozen still which
should have been open a week ago. The Great Sudbury
meadows covered with water are revealed — blue they
look over the woods — each part of the river seen further
north shines like silver in the sun — and the little pond in
the woods west of this hill is half open water. Cheering
that water with its reflections — compared with this
opaque dumb pond. How unexpectedly dumb & poor &
cold does Nature look when where we had expected to
find a glassy lake reflecting the skies and trees in the
Spring — we find only dull white ice. Such am I no doubt
to many friends — But now that I have reached the Cedar
Hill I see that there is about an acre of open water perhaps over bush island in the middle of the pond — and
there are some water-fowl there on the edge of the ice
mere black spots — though I detect their character by
discovering a relative motion. — & some are swimming
about in the water. The pond is perhaps the handsomer
after all for this distant patch only of blue water in the
midst of the field of white ice. Each enhances the other. It
is an azure spot an Elysian feature in your cold companion making the imagined concealed depths seem deeper
& rarer. This pond is worth coming to if only because it
is larger than Walden — I can so easily fancy it indefi-

nitely large — It represents to me that Icy Sea of which I have been reading in Sir J. Richardson's Book.

1 April 1852, *Journal* 4: 410–11

I see the Pond southward through the hazy atmosphere — a blue-rippled water surrounded mistily by red shrub oak woods & on one side green pines & tawny grass — A blue-rippled water surrounded by low reddish shrub oak hills — the whole invested — softened & made more remote & indistinct by a blueish mistiness. I am not sure but the contrast is more exciting & lastingly satisfactory than if the woods were green.

17 April 1852, *Journal* 4: 460

— A fine scarlet sunset. As I sit by my window & see the clouds reflected in the meadow — I think it is important to have water because it multiplies the heavens.

5 May 1852, *Journal* 5: 29

The earliest water surfaces as I remember — as soon as the ice is melted present as fair & matured scenes — as soft & warm reflecting the sky through the clear atmosphere — as in midsummer — far in advance of the earth. The earliest promise of the summer — is it not in the smooth reflecting surface of woodland lakes in which the ice is just melted? Those liquid eyes of nature — blue or black or even hazel. deep or shallow — clear or turbid. Green next the shore the color of their iris

26 June 1852, *Journal* 5: 149

The fog rises highest over the channel of the river and over the ponds in the woods which are thus revealed — I

clearly distinguish where white pond lies by this sign —
and various other ponds methinks to which I have walked
10 or 12 miles distant, & I distinguish the course of the
assabet far in the west & SW beyond the woods Every
valley is densely packed with the downy vapor — What
levelling on a great scale is done thus for the eye! The fog
rises to the top of round hill in the sudbury meadows
whose sunburnt yellow grass makes it look like a low sand
bar in the ocean and I can judge thus pretty accurately
what hills are higher than this by their elevation above the
surface of the fog. Every meadow & watercourse makes
an arm of this bay — The primeval banks make thus a
channel which only the fogs of late summer & autumn
fogs fill. The Wayland hills make a sort of promontory or
peninsula like some Nahant. If I look across thither I
think of the seamonsters that swim in that sea — & of the
wrecks that strew the bottom many fathom deep — —
where in an hour when this sea dries up farms will smile
& farmhouses be revealed. — A certain thrilling vast-
ness or wasteness it now suggests. This is one of those
ambrosial white — ever-memorable fogs presaging fair
weather — It produces the most picturesque and grandest
effects — as it rises & travels hither & thither enveloping
& concealing trees & forests & hills — It is lifted up now
into quite a little white *mt* over Fair Haven Bay and even
on its skirts only the tops of the highest pines are seen
above it — & all adown the river it has an uneven outline
like a rugged *mt* ridge in one place some rainbow tints
and far far in the S horizon, near the further verge of the
sea over Saxonville? is heaved up into great waves as if
there were breakers there. In the mean while the wood
thrush & the jay & the robin sing around me here, &

birds are heard singing from the midst of the fog. And in one short hour this sea will all evaporate & the sun be reflected from farm windows on its green bottom.

25 July 1852, Journal 5: 247–48

A pleasant time to behold a small lake in the woods is in the interval of a gentle rainstorm at this season — when the air & water are perfectly still but the sky still overcast. 1st because the lake is very smooth at such a time — 2nd as the atmosphere is so shallow & contracted — being low roofed with clouds — the lake as a lower heaven is much larger in proportion to it — With its glassy reflecting surface it is somewhat more heavenly & more full of light — than the regions of the air above it. There is a pleasing vista southward over & through a wide indentation in the hills which form its shore — where their opposite sides slope to each other so as to suggest a stream flowing from it in that direction through a wooded valley, toward some distant blue hills in Sudbury & Framingham — Goodman's & Nobscot — That is you look over & between the low near & green hills to the distant which are tinged with blue, the heavenly color. Such is what is fair to mortal eyes. In the meanwhile the wood thrush sings in the woods around the lake.

4 August 1852, Journal 5: 275–76

How rich & autumnal the haze which blues the distant hills & fills the valleys. The lakes look better in this haze which confines our view more to their reflected heavens — & makes the shore line more indistinct — Viewed from the hill top it reflects the color of the sky. Some have referred the vivid greenness next the shores to the reflection of the verdure, but it is equally green there against the RR sand bank — & in the spring before the leaves are expanded. Beyond the deep reflecting surface — near the shore where the bottom is seen it is a vivid green. I see 2 or 3 small maples already scarlet across the pond, beneath where the white stems of 3 birches diverge — at the point of a promontory next the water — a distinct scarlet tint a quarter of a mile off. Ah, many a tale their color tells of Indian times — & autumn wells — primeval dells The beautifully varied shores of Walden — The western indented with deep bays — the bold northern shore — the gracefully sweeping curve of the eastern and above all the beautifully scalloped southern shore — where successive capes overlap each other — (— and suggest unexplored coves between) Its shore is just irregular enough not to be monotonous. From this peak I can see a fish leap in almost any part of the pond — for not a pickerel or shiner picks an insect from this smooth surface but it manifestly disturbs the equilibrium of the lake — It is wonderful with what elaborateness this simple fact is advertised — this piscine murder will out — & from my distant perch I distinguish the circling undulations when they are now half a dozen rods in diameter. Methinks I distinguish Fair Haven Pond from this point — elevated by a mirage — in its seething valley like a coin in a basin. They cannot fatally injure Walden with an axe, for they have done their worst and failed. We see things in the reflection which we do not see in the substance. In the reflected woods of Pine Hill there is a vista through which I see the sky — but I am indebted to the water for this advantage — for from this point the actual wood affords no such vista.

As I look over the pond now from the eastern shore I am obliged to employ both my hands to defend my eyes against the reflected as well as the true sun — for they appear equally bright — & between my hands I look over the smooth & glassy surface of the lake — The skaters make the finest imaginable sparkle. — Otherwise it is literally as smooth as glass except where a fish leaps into the air or a swallow dips beneath its surface — Some times a fish describes an arc of 3 or 4 feet in the air — and there is a bright flash where it emerges & another where it strikes the water. A slight haze at this season makes the shore line so much the more indistinct. Looking across the pond from the Peak toward Fair Haven which I seem to see — all the earth beyond appears insulated & floated even by this small sheet of water — the heavens being seen reflected, as it were beneath it — so that it looks thin.

The scenery of this small pond is humble though very beautiful, & does not approach to grandeur, nor can it much concern one who has not long frequented it, or lived by its shore.

2 September 1852, *Journal* 5: 334–35

On Heywood's Peak by Walden. The surface is not *perfectly* smooth on account of the zephyr — & the reflections of the woods are a little indistinct and blurred. How soothing to sit on a stump on this height overlooking the pond and study the dimpling circles which are incessantly inscribed and again erased on the smooth and otherwise invisible surface, amid the reflected skies. The reflected sky is of a deeper blue How beautiful that over this vast expanse there can be no disturbance, but it is thus at once gently smoothed away & assuaged, as when a vase of water is jarred the trembling circles seek the

shore & all is smooth again. Not a fish can leap or an insect fall on it but it is reported in lines of beauty — in circling dimples — as it were the constant welling up of its
fountain — the gentle pulsing of its life — the heaving of
its breast. The thrills of joy & those of pain are indistin-
guishable. How sweet the phenomena of the lake —!
Everything that moves on its surface produces a sparkle.
The peaceful Pond! The works of men shine as in the
spring — the motion of an oar or an insect produces a
flash of light — and if an oar falls how sweet the echo.

20 September 1852, *Journal* 5: 349–50

How much more beautiful the lakes now like Fair Haven
surrounded by the autumn tinted woods & hills. — as in
an ornamented frame

2 October 1852, *Journal* 5: 365

What an ample share of the light of heaven each pond &
lake on the surface of the globe enjoys — No woods are so
dark & deep but it is light above the pond. Its window or
skylight is as broad as its surface. It lies out patent to the
sky. From the *mt* top you may not be able to see out because of the woods — but on the lake you are bathed in
light.

12 October 1852, *Journal* 5: 371

The water or lake from however distant a point seen is always the center of the landscape.

13 October 1852, *Journal* 5: 372

The pond, dark before, was now a glorious and inde-
scribable blue, mixed with dark, perhaps the opposite
side of the wave, a sort of changeable or watered-silk

blue, more cerulean if possible than the sky itself, which was now seen overhead. It required a certain division of the sight, however, to discern this. Like the colors on a steel sword-blade.

2 November 1852, *Journal* IV: 407

We find Hayward's Pond frozen five inches thick. There have been some warm suns on it, and it is handsomely marbled. I find, on looking closely, that there is an indistinct and irregular crack or cleavage in the middle of each dark mark, and I have no doubt the marbling is produced thus, *viz.*, the pond, at first all dark, cracks under a change of temperature, it is expanded and cracked in a thousand directions, and at the same time it gradually grows white as the air-bubbles expand, but wherever there is a crack in it, it interferes with the rays of heat, and the ice for a short distance on each side of it retains its original color. The forms into which the ice first cracks under a higher temperature determine the character of the marbling. This pond is bordered on the northeast with much russet sedge (?) grass beneath the bushes, and the sun, now falling on the ice, seems to slide or glance off into this grass and light it up wonderfully, filling it with yellowish light. This ice being whitened and made partially opaque by heat, while the surface is quite smooth, perhaps from new freezings then, it reflects the surrounding trees, their forms and colors, distinctly like water. The white air-bubbles are the quicksilver on the back of the mirror.

11 December 1853, *Journal* VI: 16

R.W.E. told me that W. H. Channing conjectured that the landscape looked fairer when we turned our heads, because we beheld it with nerves of the eye unused before. Perhaps this reason is worth more for suggestion than explanation. It occurs to me that the reflection of objects in still water is in a similar manner fairer than the substance, and yet we do not employ unused nerves to behold it. Is it not that we let much more light into our eyes, — which in the usual position are shaded by the brows, — in the first case by turning them more to the sky, and in the case of the reflections by having the sky placed under our feet? *i.e.* in both cases we see terrestrial objects with the sky or heavens for a background or field. Accordingly they are not dark and terrene, but lit and elysian.

11 December 1853, *Journal* VI: 17

How dead would the globe seem, especially at this season, if it were not for these water surfaces! We are slow to realize water, — the beauty and magic of it. It is interestingly strange to us forever. Immortal water, alive even in the superficies, restlessly heaving now and tossing me and my boat, and sparkling with life!

8 May 1854, *Journal* VI: 246

When, returning at 5 o'clock, I pass the pond in the road, I see the sun, which is about entering the grosser hazy atmosphere above the western horizon, brilliantly reflected in the pond, — a dazzling sheen, a bright golden shimmer. His broad sphere extended stretches the whole length of the pond toward me. First, in the extreme distance, I see a few sparkles of the gold on the dark surface; then begins a regular and solid column of shimmering gold, straight as a rule, but at one place, where a breeze strikes the surface from one side, it is remarkably spread

or widened, then recovers its straightness again, thus:
Again it is remarkably curved, say thus: then broken into
several pieces, then straight and entire again, then spread
or blown aside at the point like smoke from a chimney,
thus: Of course, if there were eyes enough to occupy all
the east shore, the whole pond would be seen as one dazzling shimmering lake of melted gold. Such beauty and
splendor adorns our walks!

19 October 1855, *Journal* VII: 499

As I sat on the high bank at the east end of Walden this afternoon, at five o'clock, I saw, by a peculiar intention or
dividing of the eye, a very striking subaqueous rainbow-
like phenomenon. A passer-by might, perhaps would,
have noticed that the bright-tinted shrubs about the high
shore on the sunny side were reflected from the water;
but, unless on the alert for such effects, he would have
failed to perceive the full beauty of the phenomenon. Unless you look for reflections, you commonly will not find
them. Those brilliant shrubs, which were from three to a
dozen feet in height, were all reflected, dimly so far as the
details of leaves, etc., were concerned, but brightly as to
color, and, of course, in the order in which they stood, —
scarlet, yellow, green, etc.; but, there being a slight ripple
on the surface, these reflections were not true to their
height though true to their breadth, but were extended
downward with mathematical perpendicularity, three or
four times too far, forming sharp pyramids of the several
colors, gradually reduced to mere dusky points. The effect of this prolongation of the reflection was a very pleasing softening and blending of the colors, especially when
a small bush of one bright tint stood directly before an-

other of a contrary and equally bright tint. It was just as if you were to brush firmly aside with your hand or a brush a fresh line of paint of various colors, or so many lumps of friable colored powders. There was, accordingly, a sort of belt, as wide as the whole height of the hill, extending downward along the whole north or sunny side of the pond, composed of exceedingly short and narrow inverted pyramids of the most brilliant colors intermixed. I have seen, indeed, similar inverted pyramids in the old drawings of tattooing about the waists of the aborigines of this country. Walden, too, like an Indian maiden, wears this broad rainbow-like belt of brilliant-colored points or cones round her waist in October. The color seems to be reflected and re-reflected from ripple to ripple, losing brightness each time by the softest possible gradation, and tapering toward the beholder, since he occupies a mere point of view. This is one of the prettiest effects of the autumnal change.

7 October 1857, *Journal* X: 74–76

Looking now toward the north side of the pond, I perceive that the reflection of the hillside seen from an opposite hill is not so broad as the hillside itself appears, owing to the different angle at which it is seen. The reflection exhibits such an aspect of the hill, *apparently,* as you would get if your eye were placed at that part of the surface of the pond where the reflection seems to be. In this instance, too, then, Nature avoids repeating herself. Not even reflections in still water are like their substances as seen by us. This, too, accounts for my seeing portions of the sky through the trees in reflections often when none appear in the substance. Is the reflection of a

hillside, however, such an aspect of it as can be obtained
by the eye directed to the hill itself from any single point
of view? It plainly is not such a view as the eye would get
looking upward from the immediate base of the hill or
water's edge, for there the first rank of bushes on the
lower part of the hill would conceal the upper. The reflection of the top appears to be such a view of it as I
should get with my eye at the water's edge above the edge
of the reflection; but would the low part of the hill also
appear from this point as it does in the reflection?
Should I see as much of the under sides of the leaves
there? If not, then the reflection is never a true copy or
repetition of its substance, but a new composition, and
this may be the source of its novelty and attractiveness,
and of this nature, too, may be the charm of an echo. I
doubt if you can ever get Nature to repeat herself exactly.

14 October 1857, *Journal* X: 96–97

Minott adorns whatever part of nature he touches;
whichever way he walks he transfigures the earth for me.
If a common man speaks of Walden Pond to me, I see only
a shallow, dull-colored body of water without reflections
or peculiar color, but if Minott speaks of it, I see the green
water and reflected hills at once, for he *has been* there.

7 November 1857, *Journal* X: 168

"These are the most exquisite delights to be found in
Greece, next to, or perhaps before, the pleasure of admir-
ing the masterpieces of art, — a little cool water under a
genial sun." I have no doubt that this is true. Why, then,
travel so far when the same pleasures may be found near
home?

3 January 1858, *Journal* X: 234–35

When I get down near to Cardinal Shore, the sun near setting, its light is wonderfully reflected from a narrow edging of yellowish stubble at the edge of the meadow ice and foot of the hill, an edging only two or three feet wide, and the stubble but a few inches high. (I am looking east.) It is remarkable because the ice is but a dull lead-color (it is so soft and sodden), reflecting no light, and the hill beyond is a dark russet, here and there patched with snow, but this narrow intermediate line of stubble is all aglow. I get its true color and brightness best when I do not look directly at it, but a little above it toward the hill, seeing it with the lower part of my eye more truly and abstractly. It is as if all the rays slid over the ice and lodged against and were reflected by the stubble. It is surprising how much sunny light a little straw that survives the winter will reflect.

4 January 1858, *Journal* X: 235–36

As I look over the smooth gleaming surface of White Pond, I am attracted by the sun-sparkles on it, as if fiery serpents were crossing to and fro. Yet if you were there you would find only insignificant insects.

As I come up from the pond, I am grateful for the fresh easterly breeze at last thickening the haze on that side and driving it in on us, for Nature must preserve her equilibrium. However, it is not much cooler.

20 October 1858, *Journal* XI: 230

We sit by the side of Little Goose Pond, which C. calls Ripple Lake or Pool, to watch the ripples on it. Now it is nearly smooth, and then there drops down on to it, deep as it lies amid the hills, a sharp and narrow blast of the icy north wind careering above, striking it, perhaps, by a point or an edge, and swiftly spreading along it, making a dark-blue ripple. Now four or five windy bolts, sharp or blunt, strike it at once and spread different ways. The boisterous but playful north wind evidently stoops from a considerable height to dally with this fair pool which it discerns beneath. You could sit there and watch these blue shadows playing over the surface like the light and shade on changeable silk, for hours. It reminds me, too, of the swift Camilla on a field [of] grain. The wind often touches the water only by the finest points or edges. It is thus when you look in some measure from the sun, but if you move round so as to come more opposite to him, then all the dark-blue ripples are all sparkles too bright to look at, for you now see the sides of the wavelets which reflect the sun to you.

9 April 1859, *Journal* XII: 128–29

Watching the ripples fall and dash across the surface of low-lying and small woodland lakes is one of the amusements of these windy March and April days. It is only on small lakes deep sunk in hollows in the woods that you can see or study them these days, for the winds sweep over the whole breadth of larger lakes incessantly, but they only touch these sheltered lakelets by fine points and edges from time to time.

9 April 1859, *Journal* XII: 129

When the playful breeze drops on the pool, it springs to right and left, quick as a kitten playing with dead leaves, clapping her paw on them. Sometimes it merely raises a single wave at one point, as if a fish darted near the surface. While to you looking down from a hillside partly from the sun, these points and dashes look thus dark-blue, almost black, they are seen by another, standing low and more opposite to the sun, as the most brilliant sheeny and sparkling surface, too bright to look at. Thus water agitated by the wind is both far brighter and far darker than smooth water, seen from this side or that, — that is, as you look at the inclined surface of the wave which reflects the sun, or at the shaded side. For three weeks past, when I have looked northward toward the flooded meadows they have looked dark-blue or black-ish, in proportion as the day was clear and the wind high from the northwest, making high waves and much shadow.

9 April 1859, *Journal* XII: 130

The mist is so thick that we cannot quite see the length of Walden as we descend to its eastern shore. The reflec-tions of the hillsides are so much the more unsubstantial, for we see even the reflected mist veiling them. You see, beneath these whitened wooded hills and shore sloping to it, the dark, half mist-veiled water. For two rods in width next the shore, where the water is shallowest and the sand bare, you see a strip of light greenish two or three rods in width, and then dark brown (with a few green streaks only) where the dark sediment of ages has accumulated. And, looking down the pond, you see on each side successive wooded promontories — with their dim reflections — growing dimmer and dimmer till they are lost in the mist. The more distant shores are a mere dusky line or film, a sort of concentration of the misti-ness.

6 December 1859, *Journal* XIII: 8–9

Seacoast

NATURE IDOLIZED
We are as near to Heaven by sea as by land.

Though there were numerous vessels at this great distance in the horizon on every side, yet the vast spaces between them, like the spaces between the stars, far as they were distant from us, so were they from one another, — nay, some were twice as far from each other as from us, — impressed us with a sense of the immensity of the ocean, the "unfruitful ocean," as it has been called, and we could see what proportion man and his works bear to the globe. As we looked off, and saw the water growing darker and darker and deeper and deeper the farther we looked, till it was awful to consider, and it appeared to have no relation to the friendly land, either as shore or bottom, — of what use is a bottom if it is out of sight, if it is two or three miles from the surface, and you are to be drowned so long before you get to it, though it were made of the same stuff with your native soil? — over that ocean, where, as the Veda says, "there is nothing to give support, nothing to rest upon, nothing to cling to," I felt that I was a land animal. The man in a balloon even may commonly alight on the earth in a few moments, but the sailor's only hope is that he may reach the distant shore. I could then appreciate the heroism of the old navigator, Sir Humphrey Gilbert, of whom it is related that, being overtaken by a storm when on his return from America, in the year 1583, far northeastward from where we were, sitting abaft with a book in his hand, just before he was swallowed up in the deep, he cried out to his comrades in the Hind, as they came within hearing, "We are as near to Heaven by sea as by land." I saw that it would not be easy to realize.

Cape Cod, 96–97

The sea-shore is a sort of neutral ground, a most advantageous point from which to contemplate this world. It is even a trivial place. The waves forever rolling to the land are too far-travelled and untamable to be familiar. Creeping along the endless beach amid the sun-squawl and the foam, it occurs to us that we, too, are the product of sea-slime.

Cape Cod, 147

The ocean is a wilderness reaching round the globe, wilder than a Bengal jungle, and fuller of monsters, washing the very wharves of our cities and the gardens of our sea-side residences.

Cape Cod, 148

NATURE IDEALIZED

The breakers looked like droves of a thousand wild horses of Neptune, rushing to the shore, with their white manes streaming far behind.

[T]hen, crossing over a belt of sand on which nothing grew, though the roar of the sea sounded scarcely louder than before, and we were prepared to go half a mile further, we suddenly stood on the edge of a bluff overlooking the Atlantic. Far below us was the beach, from half a dozen to a dozen rods in width, with a long line of breakers rushing to the strand. The sea was exceedingly dark and stormy, the sky completely overcast, the clouds still dropping rain, and the wind seemed to blow not so much as the exciting cause, as from sympathy with the already agitated ocean. The waves broke on the bars at some distance from the shore, and curving green or yellow as if over so many unseen dams, ten or twelve feet high, like a thousand waterfalls, then rolled in foam to the sand. There was nothing but that savage ocean between us and Europe.

Cape Cod, 44

The white breakers were rushing to the shore; the foam ran up the sand, and then ran back as far as we could see (and we imagined how much further along the Atlantic coast, before and behind us), as regularly, to compare great things with small, as the master of a choir beats time with his white wand; and ever and anon a higher wave caused us hastily to deviate from our path, and we looked back on our tracks filled with water and foam. The breakers looked like droves of a thousand wild horses of Neptune, rushing to the shore, with their white manes streaming far behind; and when, at length, the sun shone for a moment, their manes were rainbow-tinted. Also, the long kelp-weed was tossed up from time to time, like the tails of sea-cows sporting in the brine.

Cape Cod, 44–45

It was difficult for us landsmen to look out over the ocean without imagining land in the horizon; yet the clouds appeared to hang low over it, and rest on the water as they never do on the land, perhaps on account of the great distance to which we saw.

Cape Cod, 50

To-day the air was beautifully clear, and the sea no longer dark and stormy, though the waves still broke with foam along the beach, but sparkling and full of life. Already that morning I had seen the day break over the sea as if it came out of its bosom: —

> "The saffron-robed Dawn rose in haste from the
>   streams
> Of Ocean, that she might bring light to immortals
>   and to mortals."

The sun rose visibly at such a distance over the sea that the cloud-bank in the horizon, which at first concealed him, was not perceptible until he had risen high behind it, and plainly broke and dispersed it, like an arrow. But as yet I looked at him as rising over land, and could not, without an effort, realize that he was rising over the sea. Already I saw some vessels on the horizon, which had rounded the Cape in the night, and were now well on their watery way to other lands.

Cape Cod, 81

Still held on without a break, the inland barrens and shrubbery, the desert and the high sand-bank with its even slope, the broad white beach, the breakers, the green water on the bar, and the Atlantic Ocean; and we traversed with delight new reaches of the shore; we took another lesson in sea-horses' manes and sea-cows' tails, in sea-jellies and sea-clams, with our new-gained experience. The sea ran hardly less than the day before. It seemed with every wave to be subsiding, because such was our expectation, and yet when hours had elapsed we could see no difference. But here it was, balancing itself, the restless ocean by our side, lurching in its gait. Each wave left the sand all braided or woven, as it were, with a coarse woof and warp, and a distinct raised edge to its rapid work. We made no haste, since we wished to see the ocean at our leisure, and indeed that soft sand was no place in which to be in a hurry, for one mile there was as good as two elsewhere. Besides, we were obliged frequently to empty our shoes of the sand which one took in climbing or descending the bank.

Cape Cod, 83

To-day it was the Purple Sea, an epithet which I should not before have accepted. There were distinct patches of the color of a purple grape with the bloom rubbed off. But first and last the sea is of all colors. Well writes Gilpin concerning "the brilliant hues which are continually playing on the surface of a quiet ocean," and this was not too turbulent at a distance from the shore. "Beautiful," says he, "no doubt in a high degree are those glimmering tints which often invest the tops of mountains; but they are mere coruscations compared with these marine colors, which are continually varying and shifting into each other in all the vivid splendor of the rainbow, through the space often of several leagues." Commonly, in calm weather, for half a mile from the shore, where the bottom tinges it, the sea is green, or greenish, as are some ponds; then blue for many miles, often with purple tinges, bounded in the distance by a light almost silvery stripe; beyond which there is generally a dark-blue rim, like a mountain-ridge in the horizon, as if, like that, it owed its color to the intervening atmosphere. On another day it will be marked with long streaks, alternately smooth and rippled, light-colored and dark, even like our inland meadows in a freshet, and showing which way the wind sets.

Thus we sat on the foaming shore, looking on the wine-colored ocean, — ... Here and there was a darker spot on its surface, the shadow of a cloud, though the sky was so clear that no cloud would have been noticed otherwise, and no shadow would have been seen on the land, where a much smaller surface is visible at once. So, distant clouds and showers may be seen on all sides by a sailor in the course of a day, which do not necessarily portend rain where he is.

Cape Cod, 93–94

The light-house lamps were still burning, though now with a silvery lustre, when I rose to see the sun come out of the Ocean; for he still rose eastward of us; but I was convinced that he must have come out of a dry bed beyond that stream, though he seemed to come out of the water.

> "The sun once more touched the fields,
> Mounting to heaven from the fair flowing
> Deep-running Ocean."

Cape Cod, 139

We wished to associate with the Ocean until it lost the pond-like look which it wears to a countryman. We still thought that we could see the other side. Its surface was still more sparkling than the day before, and we beheld "the countless smilings of the ocean waves"; though some of them were pretty broad grins, for still the wind blew and the billows broke in foam along the beach. The nearest beach to us on the other side, whither we looked, due east, was on the coast of Galicia, in Spain, whose capital is Santiago, though by old poets' reckoning it should have been Atlantis or the Hesperides; but heaven is found to be farther west now.

Cape Cod, 140

Further Reading

___

WORKS BY THOREAU

NOTE ON TEXTS: For nearly a century the standard edition has been *The Writings of Henry David Thoreau,* edited by Bradford Torrey and Francis H. Allen, 20 volumes (Boston: Houghton Mifflin, 1906), volumes VII to XX of which comprise the *Journal* (separately numbered I to XIV). The 1906 Houghton Mifflin edition is being superseded by the ongoing *The Writings of Henry D. Thoreau* (Princeton, N.J.: Princeton University Press, 1971–), which among other titles has published five volumes of the *Journal* to date. The Princeton edition of the *Journal* prints Thoreau's text exactly as it appears in manuscript and retains all peculiarities of his spelling, punctuation, and syntax. In "The Spirit of Thoreau" series, arabic numerals indicate the five volumes of the Princeton edition; roman numerals, the volumes of the 1906 *Journal* not yet superseded by Princeton.

Cape Cod. Edited by Joseph J. Moldenhauer. Princeton: Princeton University Press, 1988.
The Correspondence of Henry David Thoreau. Edited by

Walter Harding and Carl Bode. New York: New York University Press, 1958.

The Maine Woods. Edited by Joseph J. Moldenhauer. Princeton: Princeton University Press, 1972.

The Natural History Essays. Edited by Robert Sattelmeyer. Salt Lake City: Peregrine Smith, 1980.

Walden. Edited by J. Lyndon Shanley. Princeton: Princeton University Press, 1971.

A Week on the Concord and Merrimack Rivers. Edited by Carl F. Hovde, William Howarth, and Elizabeth Hall Witherell. Princeton: Princeton University Press, 1980.

The Writings of Henry David Thoreau. V: *Excursions and Poems.* Boston: Houghton Mifflin, 1906.

WORKS ABOUT THOREAU

The following sources were instrumental in formulating the ideas contained within the introduction, and to these scholars I am extremely grateful.

Bonner, Willard H. *Harp on the Shore: Thoreau and the Sea.* Albany: State University of New York Press, 1985.

Channing, William Ellery *Thoreau: The Poet-Naturalist.* Boston: Roberts Brothers, 1873.

Friesen, Victor C. *The Spirit of the Huckleberry: Sensuousness in Henry Thoreau.* Edmonton: University of Alberta Press, 1984.

Garber, Frederick. *Thoreau's Redemptive Imagination.* New York: New York University Press, 1977.

Harding, Walter. *The Days of Henry Thoreau: A Biography.* New York: Dover Publications, 1982.

Hildebidle, John. *Thoreau. A Naturalist's Liberty.* Cambridge, Mass.: Harvard University Press, 1983.

McGregor, Robert K. *A Wider View of the Universe: Henry Thoreau's Study of Nature.* Champaign: University of Illinois Press, 1997.

McIntosh, James. *Thoreau as Romantic Naturalist: His Shifting Stance Toward Nature.* Ithaca: Cornell University Press, 1974.

Milder, Robert. *Reimagining Thoreau.* Cambridge, Eng.: Cambridge University Press, 1995.

Paul, Sherman. *The Shores of America: Thoreau's Inward Exploration.* Champaign: University of Illinois Press, 1958.

Pedersen, Ken. *Walden: Repose, Inspiration, Peace.* Pennsauken, N.J.: Symark.

Richardson, Robert D., Jr. *Henry Thoreau: A Life of the Mind.* Berkeley:. University of California Press, 1998.

Walker, Marianne. "Thoreau and the Art of Seeing." *Concord Saunterer* 15 (Spring 1980), 10–14.

Walls, Laura D. *Seeing New Worlds: Henry David Thoreau and Nineteenth-Century Natural Science.* Madison: University of Wisconsin Press, 1995.

Wilson, Eric. "Thoreau, Thales, and the Distribution of Water." *Concord Saunterer* 6, new series, (1998): 27–44.

Worster, Donald. *Nature's Economy: A History of Ecological Ideas.* Cambridge, Eng.: Cambridge University Press, 1977.

Related Works

France, Robert L. "Gaian Integrity: A Clarion Precept for Global Preservation." *Trumpeter* 9 (Spring 1992), 159–64.

Lopez, Barry. *Crossing Open Ground.* New York: Random House, 1989.

Olson, Sigurd F. *Listening Point.* Minneapolis: University of Minnesota Press, 1997.

Raban, Jonathan. *Passage to Juneau: A Sea and Its Meanings.* New York: Pantheon Books, 1999.

Roszak, Theodore. *The Voice of the Earth: An Exploration of Ecopsychology.* New York: Touchstone Books, 1992.

Schama, Simon. *Landscape and Memory.* Toronto: Random House, 1995.

Sewall, Laura. "Reversing the World." *Orion* (Autumn 1999): 19–24.

——. *Sight and Sensibility: The Ecopsychology of Perception.* New York: Penguin Putnam, 1999.

——. "The Skill of Ecological Perception." In Roszak, Theodore, Mary E. Gomes, and Allen D. Kanner, eds. *Ecopsychology: Restoring the Earth, Healing the Mind.* San Francisco: Sierra Club Books, 1995.

Weiss, A. S. *Unnatural Horizons: Paradox and Contradiction in Landscape Architecture.* Princeton: Princeton Architectural Press, 1997.

Acknowledgments

———

Special thanks to Leslie Zucker for manuscript preparation, encouragement, and life lessons in integrating poetry and science toward protecting rivers.

> I sailed up a river with a pleasant wind,
> New lands, new people, and new thoughts to find;
> Many fair reaches and headlands appeared,
> And many dangers were there to be feared;
> But when I remember where I have been,
> And the fair landscapes that I have seen,
> THOU seemest the only permanent shore,
> The cape never rounded, nor wandered o'er.
>
> —Thoreau's dedication in *A Week on
> the Concord and Merrimack Rivers*

THE SPIRIT OF THOREAU

"How many a man has dated a new era in his life from the reading of a book," wrote Henry David Thoreau in *Walden*. Today that book, perhaps more than any other American work, continues to provoke, inspire, and change lives all over the world, and each rereading is fresh and challenging. Yet as Thoreau's countless admirers know, there is more to the man than *Walden*. An engineer, poet, teacher, naturalist, lecturer, and political activist, he truly had several lives to lead, and each one speaks forcefully to us today.

The Spirit of Thoreau introduces the thoughts of a great writer on a variety of important topics, some that we readily associate him with, some that may be surprising. Each book includes selections from his familiar published works as well as from less well known and even previously unpublished lectures, letters, and journal entries. Thoreau claimed that "to read well, that is, to read true books in a true spirit, is a noble exercise, and one that will task the reader more than any exercise which the customs of the day esteem." The volume editors and the Thoreau Society believe that you will find these new aspects of Thoreau an exciting "exercise" indeed.

This Thoreau Society series reunites Henry Thoreau with

his historic publisher. For more than a hundred years, the venerable publishing firm of Houghton Mifflin has been associated with standard editions of the works of Emerson and Thoreau and with important bibliographical and interpretive studies of the New England transcendentalists. Until Princeton University Press began issuing new critical texts in *The Writings of Henry D. Thoreau,* beginning with *Walden* in 1971, Thoreauvians were well served by Houghton Mifflin's twenty-volume edition of *The Writings of Henry David Thoreau* (1906). Having also published Walter Harding's annotated edition of *Walden* (1995), Houghton Mifflin is again in the forefront of Thoreau studies.

You are invited to continue exploring Thoreau by joining our society. For well over fifty years we have presented publications, annual gatherings, and other programs to further the appreciation of Thoreau's thought and writings. And now we have embarked on a bold new venture. In partnership with the Walden Woods Project, the Thoreau Society has formed the Thoreau Institute, a research and educational center housing the world's greatest collection of materials by and about Thoreau. In ways that the author of *Walden* could not have imagined, his message is still changing lives in a brand-new era.

For membership information, write to the Thoreau Society, 44 Baker Farm, Lincoln, MA 01773-3004, or call 781-259-4750. To learn more about the Thoreau Institute, write to the same address; call 781-259-4700; or visit the Web site: www.walden.org.

WESLEY T. MOTT
Series Editor
The Thoreau Society